A FIRST RUSSIAN VOC

C000231226

Patrick Waddington

A FIRST RUSSIAN VOCABULARY

PATRICK WADDINGTON

RUSSIAN
STUDIES

PUBLISHED BY BRISTOL CLASSICAL PRESS
GENERAL EDITOR: JOHN H. BETTS
RUSSIAN TEXTS SERIES EDITOR:
NEIL CORNWELL

This impression 2008
This edition published in 1992 by
Bristol Classical Press
an imprint of
Gerald Duckworth & Co. Ltd.
90-93 Cowcross Street, London EC1M 6BF
Tel: 020 7490 7300
Fax: 020 7490 0080
info@duckworth-publishers.co.uk
www.ducknet.co.uk

First published in 1988 by Basil Blackwell Ltd.
© Patrick Waddington, 1988, 1992

A catalogue record for this book is available
from the British Library

ISBN 978 1 85399 248 3

Printed and bound in Great Britain by
CPI Antony Rowe, Eastbourne

CONTENTS

PREFACE

I

A First Russian Vocabulary replaces and vastly expands a work originally published by Bradda Books a quarter of a century ago and until recently in print: *A First Thousand Russian Words*. Like its predecessor, it has two distinct functions. First, it gives all necessary information on some 2300 words considered most important for various purposes like travel to the Soviet Union, conversation with Russians, elementary essay-writing, the reading of simple literature, and success in school examinations. The most basic words, some 835 in all, are listed again without meanings at the end in order that students may test themselves; they must, of course, always be checked against the main entries. Secondly, the Vocabulary is an essential companion to Blackwell Russian Texts, which will in future exclude from their own glossaries all words here included except where they show different senses. This is why *A First Russian Vocabulary* has had to be arranged alphabetically rather than by categories.

In compiling the book I have drawn upon and closely compared many existing Russian vocabularies, frequency dictionaries, and grammar-books both traditional and modern, as well as all readily available lists of words prescribed by education authorities in

Britain, the USA and New Zealand. The scope and purpose of these sources vary greatly and their choice of vocabulary likewise. Some words will always choose themselves; others are common to most lists; but yet others must depend on specific preferences or needs. The last group is naturally the most difficult and controversial to establish. Some reflections on the problems involved will be found in Part II of this Preface, if you care to read that far. For the present Vocabulary many hard decisions have needed to be made in accepting or rejecting words from an originally much larger pool. The final selection is my own, and I am therefore responsible for any supposed errors of judgment as well as for matters of fact, but I have received invaluable help and advice from expert friends and colleagues. Among these I must thank with especial warmth Mr Stephen Marder, Mr Michael Holman and Mrs Irene Hughes who prepared the text for publication.

Entries in *A First Russian Vocabulary* are presented in accordance with a general principle, namely that only those features of a word which may be considered basic should be included in explanation of it. This applies equally to meaning, morphology and stress patterns. It seems pointless, for example, to give the first and second persons singular of течь, 'to flow', or to state that кошка may mean 'grapnel' or 'crampon' as well as 'cat'. Essential irregularities of form or stress are entered in the manner explained below.

VERBS are listed first in the imperfective infinitive. In a very few instances the perfective only is shown; this is always clearly stated. Where the perfective is formed from the imperfective by the addition of a prefix, the latter is entered after an oblique stroke: читать/про-. Other aspectual pairs are printed in full unless contraction is clear: помогать/помочь, but объяснять/-нить. Where two different perfectives apply, they appear thus: говорить/ по- *and* сказать; reference is then made in the English part of the entry to the respective meaning of each (*1st pf., 2nd pf.*). If a verb has any irregularity of conjugation or stress, this is shown in brackets after the infinitive concerned, save that, where the difference between the aspects is purely prefixal, the irregularities are shown after the infinitive pair and must be adjusted for the perfective. (See, for instance, писа́ть/на-, where на- must be added to пишу́ пи́шешь in the perfective future tense and to писа́л, etc., in the past. It should also be pointed out here that perfective forms in вы́- retain constant stress on the prefix; see, for instance, расти́/вы́-.) Bracketed information may concern the present (or perfective future) tense, the past tense, and the imperative. The first and second persons singular of the present (or perfective future) tense, and if necessary also its third person plural, are given as models wherever the conjugation shows any irregularity of ending or stress: терпе́ть/по- (терплю́ те́рпишь). Where a verb is used primarily or exclusively in the third person, this is indicated instead. Irregular forms in the past tense are set out in the masculine and feminine, thus: вёл вела́ (from вести́, under води́ть). If the plural stress is different from the feminine, it too is given; the neuter stress is always consistent with the plural. When, as quite often happens, a past tense is perfectly regular except for a feminine end stress, this alone is given, thus: врала́ (from врать). Occasionally, alternative stresses are indicated: пе́реда́л(и) передала́ (which must be understood as: пе́редал or переда́л, пе́редали(-о) or переда́ли(-о), *but* передала́ only). Please note finally that, if a verb has quite different meanings in English according to the constructions used after it, both the constructions and the meanings may be found separated by a semi-colon (see for instance дава́ть); otherwise, alternative constructions are usually indicated by an oblique line (see for instance игра́ть).

NOUNS of standard declension types are listed in the nominative singular alone if their spelling and stress remain perfectly regular. Any change in the genitive singular which is then maintained throughout is indicated thus: америка́нец (-а́нца), моря́к (-яка́). The genitive singular is also shown for nouns derived from adjectives: моро́женое (-ого), столо́вая (-ой). Where in a feminine noun the stress alters for the accusative only, both this and the genitive case are indicated: борода́ (бо́роду -ы́). Other irregular singular parts are given as appropriate. In the plural, a stress change valid throughout is generally indicated in the nominative only, thus: колесо́ (*pl.* колёса). A stress change in the nominative plural accompanied by an irregularity of form or spelling is, however, expressed thus: ве́чер (*pl.* -а́ -о́в). Both the nominative and the genitive, and if necessary the dative, are indicated also where the plural stress is not constant, where there may be any doubt, or where a combination of irregularities occurs: вор (*pl.* во́ры -о́в), слеза́ (*pl.* слёзы слёз слеза́м), о́блако (*pl.* -а́ -о́в -а́м). A genitive plural fill-vowel is always shown: посы́лка (*G pl.* -лок), спа́льня (*G pl.* спа́лен). This phenomenon is often found in the feminine form of a masculine and feminine pair; in order to save space, брюне́т and брюне́тка, for example, are entered thus: брюне́т/-ка (*G pl.* -ток). As with verbs, alternative stresses are occasionally found: стена́ (... сте́нам). Note, finally, that the instructions '*no pl.*' or '*use s. only*', given as appropriate with certain words like шокола́д and пече́нье, should be taken as guides to usage at this level: they are not in all cases absolute.

ADJECTIVES in Russian, with few exceptions, are far more commonly found in their long forms than in their short ones. Many have no short forms at all: such are ру́сский, настоя́щий, деревя́нный. Some (for instance бе́лый, мёртвый) have short forms which occur in literature or in fixed expressions, but to indicate these in a basic vocabulary would be wrong. However, a particular problem arises where some irregularity of spelling or stress occurs. If short forms do exist and are reasonably often used, not to show them at all might wrongly imply that they are regularly derived. Given also that the stress in short comparative adjectives (usually identical in form with comparative adverbs) generally follows that of the feminine short form, it frequently seemed best to put such irregularities in rather than to leave them out. Where the short feminine form alone of a given adjective shows a change of stress, it only is indicated: ста́рый (стара́). Where other forms show irregularity of stress or spelling, they also are given. Sometimes it is enough to show the masculine and feminine: прия́тный (-тен -тна); sometimes the plural also needs to be given: просто́й (про́ст(ы)-а́). Neuter short forms in -o (and thus impersonal forms and **ADVERBS**) may be taken to be derived regularly from adjectives if no information is given or if the feminine short form only is indicated: опа́сный will give опа́сно, твёрдый (тверда́) will give твёрдо. If the plural form in -ы (-и) is shown, then the neuter adjective or adverb will follow its stress unless otherwise stated: горя́чий (-ча́ -чи́) gives горячо́, and просто́й (see above) gives про́сто. In order to avoid possible confusion, however, many of the commonest Russian adverbs are listed separately even when regularly formed from long adjectives according to these rules. Irregular comparative adjectives and adverbs are also given where sufficiently common, as well as irregular superlatives.

    CROSS-REFERENCE has been kept to a minimum, in order to save space. A few entries were essential, such as (сказа́ть: *see* говори́ть), (лю́ди: *see* челове́к), and several others seemed advisable for various reasons. Help is also given in contrasting words (like о́тпуск and кани́кулы) or in linking them together (as with с and на). However, no cross-reference is made in the case of perfectives formed from imperfectives by prefix (in this Vocabulary by вы-, за-, из-/ис-, на-, по-, под(о)-, при-, раз-/рас-, с(о)- and у-). Nor is separate identification given for compounds of идти́, which need to be looked up directly under their imperfective forms in -ходи́ть; this is true not only of infinitives (войти́, подойти́, and so on) but also of other verb forms (such as войду́ or подошла́). Indeed, no cross reference at all is made of a purely inflexional kind (like кем то кто, двухсо́т to две́сти, and so on). To have made entries for all these would have vastly increased the length of the Vocabulary without, I believe, adding much of practical use. The only other important thing to note in this connection is that all words here included which are formed with -то or -нибудь are listed together under the entry -то. That this is not completely logical will be obvious; but it should increase intelligibility.

    One feature of this Vocabulary which distinguishes it from most other British word-lists, including those prescribed for examination purposes, is that it contains **AMERICAN** terminology where appropriate. It seemed unnecessary to give American spellings (such as 'labor', 'kilometer') or convenience forms (like 'fry-pan' for 'frying-pan'), but the commonest words not in British usage are incorporated ('the fall', 'sidewalk', and so on), as well as some vocabulary which Americans might need in order to avoid confusion with British usage (for instance, 'pants' and 'purse').

Please note that no indication of any kind is given as to the **PRONUNCIATION** of Russian words. This must be studied with the teacher or through a good grammar book or oral language course.

II

For those who are interested to read on, it should be pointed out that the two aims outlined at the beginning of this Preface differ very greatly from each other and are to some extent even in conflict. Many words occurring frequently in Russian texts, especially in pre-Revolutionary ones, cannot reasonably be incorporated in a modern basic vocabulary: such, for instance, are мужик ('peasant'), грех ('sin') and топóр ('axe'). On the other hand, many words actually included here will feature in few texts chosen for the Blackwell series and yet have obvious value for tourists or for students of contemporary Soviet culture: such, for example, are коньяк, джинсы and поп-музыка. Correspondingly, the selection of some other words like крикет and бейсбóл can be justified only because this Vocabulary will, after all, be used in English-speaking countries where such concepts are accorded importance. A certain counter-balance has been sought by the inclusion of significant Soviet terminology like коллектив, комсомóлец and бригáда. It may seem risky to incorporate Soviet words which are currently in vogue but could easily disappear. Some may assert, for instance, that гласность and перестрóйка are not basic. Let us only hope that they are . . .

It is for considerations like these that any Russian word-list, to be useful, must in some degree be personal and arbitrary. Only those who have attempted to compare different vocabularies will know quite what astonishing variations they may show. It is, moreover, a mistake to believe that such problems can be overcome by present scientific means. The value of frequency-lists is limited, since everything depends on their purpose, input and technique. A brief assessment of the more famous ones could be of value here. Full references are given in the Bibliography that follows the Preface.

Josselson, a pioneer in the field, examined 134 samples from Russian literature in the period 1830–1948, covering primarily fiction but also journalism, literary criticism and a little drama. He chose from these some 5230 significant words and divided them into six lists of relative frequency. By contrast, Šteinfeldt extracted the approximately 2500 commonest words in 350 items of Soviet fiction and drama, chiefly works for children. Vakar, believing his predecessors to have paid inadequate attention to the spoken, adult word, investigated the dialogue of 93 plays published between 1957 and 1966 and extracted a meaningful but modest core of 360 words. Finally, Zasorina and her team examined roughly equal percentages of texts by Soviet prose-writers, dramatists, journalists, and scientific and other publicist authors, arranging the almost 40,000 different words there found in an impressive-looking dictionary, reprinting also in order of frequency the first 9000 of them. And what is the result? Some words in Vakar's 360 are not found at all in Šteinfeldt's 2500. Šteinfeldt's list includes май but not декабрь, воскресéнье but not понедéльник, четы́рнадцать but not трина́дцать, and so on, but on the other hand finds room for words like прибалти́йский ('Baltic', adj.) which fail by a long way to make Zasorina's first 9000. Zasorina, meanwhile, gives поли́ция and полицéйский as being far commoner than мили́ция and милиционéр, and америка́нский as having a definite edge on ру́сский! Her own first 360 words or so include items as improbable as ка́тер ('launch'), yet she rates well outside her first 9000 оби́деть ('to offend'), included in Vakar's 360. The integrity of all these scholars is beyond question, and Vakar, in particular, is very sensitive to the problems raised by his research; but there is clearly something wrong somewhere. Partly it is a matter of the relatively few texts chosen (when compared to the millions available), or quirkish selection of texts (Zasorina's team included works by Lenin published in 1919 in a study otherwise devoted to writings since 1940). Partly it is that insufficient prominence is often given to range of use as opposed to nominal frequency. Partly there is the technical difficulty of knowing whether some individual 'words' are actually two, or even three or more, depending on their grammatical form or their sense, or whether, on the contrary, two or more 'words' may be one: given that most Soviet linguists, at least, tend to split an imperfective and perfective pair in two for the purposes of counting, each will occupy a far lower place in frequency ranking than would be the case if the two were put together. The main deficiency, however, is that no one yet has had the resources or technology to study exhaustively the actual spoken vocabulary of large numbers of representative native Russian speakers, as opposed to the words that just a few of them sometimes write down.

What may one conclude from all this? First, that frequency-lists need to be checked against commonsense observations. Their findings do not coincide for any but the most obviously important words (perhaps between 100 and 150), and after a certain point (perhaps about 300 words) they begin to diverge too sharply to be given anything but the most cautious emphasis. Secondly, certain word clusters cannot be broken up in the way which frequency counts must necessarily treat them: it would be absurd, for example, to exclude from a basic vocabulary some months of the year, days of the week, essential numerals, and so on, simply on the grounds that some researcher or other had not come across them often in a certain selection of texts. (This is not at all to say, of course, that such findings are not interesting, sociologically as well as linguistically.) Thirdly, care must be taken to include words of significant value to all kinds of expected users: the trouble with frequency counts is precisely that they cater for only *some* users. Fourthly, it is evident that after about 1000 words, and perhaps well before, practically any new words chosen could be matched by others claiming equal consideration, depending on the team or individual choosing them and on the point of view. One could consciously make the vocabulary more Soviet, more traditional, more universal, more scholarly, more popular, more touristy or more eclectic. I have followed this last course, with the restriction (or perhaps advantage) of an alphabetical vocabulary which cannot reasonably aim for completeness within any predetermined categories of words.

Finally, I wish to express my regret that, for reasons of economy, it has not been possible to set the Vocabulary in separate Russian and English columns. To have done so would have allowed entries to be more easily learnt and checked. It is only to be hoped that users of the book will find the present dictionary-style layout of words both easy to follow and pleasant on the eye.

Patrick Waddington
Wellington, New Zealand
28 June 1988

BIBLIOGRAPHY

Note: Many other works besides those listed were consulted, including all the best-known grammar books and all available word-lists prescribed by examining and other academic authorities in Britain, the USA and New Zealand. This bibliography includes only those published dictionaries and vocabularies which were found most consistently useful as a basis for the presentation of chosen entries in *A First Russian Vocabulary*.

Ageenko, F. L., and Zarva, M. V., *Slovar' udarenii dlya rabotnikov radio i televideniya*, ed. D. E. Rozental', 5th ed., Moscow, 1984.

Anpilogova, V. G., Vladimirskii, E. Yu., Zimin, V. I., and Sosenko, E. Yu., *Essential Russian–English Dictionary*, Moscow, [1962?]; 2nd ed., 1973.

Avanesov, R. I. (ed.), *Orfoepicheskii slovar' russkogo yazyka. Proiznoshenie, udarenie, grammaticheskie formy*, Moscow, 1983.

Avanesov, R. I., and Ozhegov, S. I. (eds), *Russkoe literaturnoe proiznoshenie i udarenie*, Moscow, 1959.

Falla, P. S. (ed.), *The Oxford English–Russian Dictionary*, Oxford, 1984.

Hermenau, Otto (ed.), *Wortschatzminimum für den Russischunterricht in der zehnklassigen allgemeinbildenden polytechnischen Oberschule*, Berlin, 1960.

Josselson, Harry H., *The Russian Word Count and Frequency Analysis of Grammatical Categories of Standard Literary Russian*, Detroit, 1953.

Langenscheidt's Russian–English English–Russian Dictionary, with special emphasis on American English, Berlin, Munich and London, 1964.

Leksicheskii minimum po russkomu yazyku dlya studentov-inostrantsev pervogo goda obucheniya, Moscow, [1961].

Markov, Yu., and Vishnyakova, T., 'Russkaya razgovornaya rech': 1200 naibolee upotrebitel'nykh slov', *Russkii yazyk v natsional'noi shkole*, 1965, no. 6, pp. 27–34.

Müller, V. K., *Anglo–russkii slovar'*, 20th ed., Moscow, 1985.

Shanskii, N. M. (ed.), *4000 naibolee upotrebitel'nykh slov russkogo yazyka. Uchebnyi slovar' dlya zarubezhnykh shkol*, Moscow, 1978.

Slovar' russkogo yazyka, 2nd ed., 4 vols, Moscow: AN SSSR, 1981–4.

Slovar' sovremennogo russkogo literaturnogo yazyka, 17 vols, Moscow and Leningrad: AN SSSR, 1950–65.

Smirnitskii, A. I., *Russko–angliiskii slovar'*, 13th ed., ed. O. S. Akhmanova, Moscow, 1985.

Šteinfeldt, E., *Russian Word Count: 2500 words most commonly used in modern literary Russian; guide for teachers of Russian*, Moscow, [1965?].

Vakar, N. P., *A Word Count of Spoken Russian: the Soviet usage*, Ohio State University Press, 1966.

Waddington, Patrick, *A Basic Russian–English Vocabulary*, London, 1962.

—— *A First Thousand Russian Words*, London, 1963, etc.

—— *Russian by Subjects*, Letchworth, 1965, etc. (Bradda Books); Oxford, 1984 (Basil Blackwell).

Wheeler, Marcus, *The Oxford Russian–English Dictionary*, Oxford, 1972; 2nd ed., 1984.

Wilson, Elizabeth A. M., *The Modern Russian Dictionary for English Speakers* (*English–Russian*), Oxford and Moscow, 1982.

Zasorina, L. N. (ed.), *Chastotnyi slovar' russkogo yazyka*, Moscow, 1977.

LIST OF ABBREVIATIONS

A	accusative case	*inf.*	infinitive
adj.	adjective	*interrog.*	interrogative
adv.	adverb	*intrans.*	intransitive
Amer.	American (usage)	*m.*	masculine
coll.	colloquial	*n.*	neuter
comp.	comparative	*N*	nominative case
cond.	conditional	*neg.*	negative
conj.	conjunction	*nn.*	noun
D	dative case	*P*	prepositional case
def.	definite (determinate)	*pers.*	person(s)
Eng.	English	*pf.*	perfective aspect
esp.	especially	*pl.*	plural
f.	feminine	*prep.*	preposition
fut.	future	*pres.*	present
G	genitive case	*pron.*	pronoun
I	instrumental case	*refl.*	reflexive
imp.	imperative	*rel.*	relative
impf.	imperfective aspect	*s.*	singular
incl.	including	*sb.*	somebody
indecl.	indeclinable	*sth.*	something
indef.	indefinite	*subj.*	subject
	(indeterminate)	*subjunct.*	subjunctive

| *superl.* | superlative | *transl.* | translated (as) |
| *trans.* | transitive | *usu.* | usually |

Conventional Signs

* denotes that the declension of a word so marked must be looked up in a grammar book.

/ is used to differentiate between the imperfective and perfective forms of verbs and between the masculine and feminine forms of noun pairs; to save space in a series of usages and definitions; and to balance alternative constructions in the Russian and the English parts of a given entry.

VOCABULARY

a and/but (*stands in sense between* **и** *and* **но**)

он ру́сский, а я америка́нка he is Russian, and/but I am American

я не меха́ник, а инжене́р I'm not a mechanic; I'm an engineer

а то *or* **а не то** or (else), otherwise; for, because

ава́рия accident, crash; breakdown

потерпе́ть ава́рию to have an accident, crash

а́вгуст August

авиаписьмо́ (*pl.* **-пи́сьма -пи́сем**) aerogramme, air letter

авиапо́чта airmail

авиапо́чтой *or* **а́виа** by air(mail)

австрали́ец (**-и́йца**) Australian (*male*)

австрали́йка (*G pl.* **-и́ек**) Australian (*female*)

австрали́йский Australian (*adj.*)

Австра́лия Australia

авто́бус bus, coach

е́хать на авто́бусе to go by bus

автома́т (*see also* **телефо́н**) vending/slot machine, coin box, coin-op

автомоби́ль *m.* car, (*Amer.*) automobile

а́втор author

автостра́да *or* **автомагистра́ль** *f.* motorway, trunk-road, (*Amer.*) freeway, superhighway

а́дрес (*pl.* **-а́ -о́в**) address

по а́дресу at/to the right address

не по а́дресу at/to the wrong address

а́збука alphabet

азиа́тский Asiatic, Asian (*adj.*)

А́зия Asia

аккура́тный (**-тен -тна**) accurate;

1

punctual; tidy, neat, careful, painstaking

актёр actor, player

актри́са actress

алле́я avenue (*in country or city*); lane, path (*in park*)

алло́! hallo (*telephone greeting*)

альпини́зм climbing, mountaineering

Аме́рика America

америка́нец (-а́нца) American (*male*)

америка́нка (*G pl.* **-нок**) American (*female*)

америка́нский American (*adj.*)

англи́йский English (*adj.*)

англи́йский язы́к English (language; *see also* **по-**)

англича́нин (*pl.* **-а́не -а́н**) English(man) (*pl.* the English)

англича́нка (*G pl.* **-нок**) English(woman)

А́нглия England, (*for Russians also*) Britain

анке́та questionnaire, (enquiry) form

апельси́н orange

аппети́т appetite

прия́тного аппети́та! enjoy your meal, bon appétit

апре́ль *m.* April

апте́ка chemist's (shop), pharmacy, (*Amer.*) drugstore, druggist('s)

ара́бский Arabic, Arab (*adj.*)

арбу́з water-melon

а́рмия army

арти́ст /-ка (*G pl.* **-ток**) artist(e), performer, actor (actress),

entertainer (*singer, dancer, musician, etc.*)

Атланти́ческий океа́н the Atlantic (Ocean)

атле́тика athletics, athletic sports

а́томный atomic, nuclear, nuclear-powered

аттеста́т certificate

аттеста́т о сре́днем образова́нии (*coll.* **аттеста́т зре́лости**) school-leaving certificate, (*Amer.*) high school diploma (*enabling entry to higher education*)

афи́ша poster, playbill, notice

А́фрика Africa

аэропо́рт (в аэропорту́) airport

ба́бушка (*G pl.* **-шек**) grandmother, granny, grandma

бага́ж (-а́) luggage, bags, baggage

ба́за base (*military, tourist, etc.*)

балала́йка (*G pl.* **-а́ек**) balalaika (*Russian musical instrument*)

балери́на ballet dancer (ballerina)

бале́т ballet

балко́н balcony

Балти́йское мо́ре the Baltic (Sea)

бана́н banana

банк bank (*for money, data*)

ба́нка (*G pl.* **ба́нок**) jar; tin, can

бар bar, snack bar

бараба́н drum

баскетбо́л basketball

ба́шня (*G pl.* **ба́шен**) tower

бая́н bayan (*Russian musical instrument*)

бе́гать to run (*indef.*)

бежа́ть/по- (**бегу́ бежи́шь бегу́т**) to run (*def.*)
беда́ trouble, misfortune
что за беда́! so what? what does/can it matter?
бе́дный (**-ден -дна́ -дны**) poor
без (+ *G*) without; to (*the hour*)
без пяти́ (**мину́т**) **час** (it is) five (minutes) to one; at five to one
без че́тверти шесть (it is) a quarter to six; at (a) quarter to six
безрабо́тный (**-тен -тна**) unemployed, out of work
бейсбо́л baseball
бе́лка (*G pl.* **бе́лок**) squirrel
белоку́рый fair(-haired), blond(e)
бе́лый white
бельё washing, laundry, linen (articles), clothes (*to be washed or ironed*)
(**ни́жнее**) **бельё** underwear
бензи́н petrol, (*Amer.*) gas(oline)
бензоколо́нка (*G pl.* **-нок**; *use* **на**) petrol station, (*Amer.*) gas station, filling station
бе́рег (**на берегу́**; *pl.* **-а́ -о́в**) bank, shore, coast, side (*of river, lake, sea*)
береги́сь/береги́тесь! (*from* **бере́чься**) (+ *G*) watch out! look out! take care! mind! beware (*of sth.*)!
берёза birch(-tree)
Берёзка Beriozka shop (*where export-quality goods are bought in hard foreign currencies*)

бесе́да chat, talk, conversation; discussion
бесе́довать/по- (**-дую -дуешь**) to chat, talk, *etc.*
беспла́тный (**-тен -тна**) free (of charge), gratuitous
беспла́тно (*adv.*) free, gratis, for nothing
беспоко́ить/по- *or* **о-** to worry, disturb, bother, trouble (*sb.*)
беспоко́иться, *etc.* to worry, be worried/uneasy/anxious, to bother, trouble (oneself)
бесполе́зный (**-зен -зна**) useless
библиоте́ка library
биле́т ticket; pass (*on public transport, etc.*); (ID/ membership) card
биоло́гия biology
бить/по- (**бью бьёшь**; *imp.* **бей(те)**)) to beat
би́ться, *etc.* (**с** + *I*) to fight (with/against *sb.*)
бифште́кс (beef)steak
благодари́ть/по- to thank
благодарю́ вас thank you (*more formal than* **спаси́бо**)
благода́рный (**-рен -рна**) thankful, grateful
благодаря́ (+ *D*) thanks to, owing to, because of
бланк form (*to be filled in*)
бле́дный (**-ден -дна́ -дны**) pale
бли́зкий (**-зок -зка́ -зки**; *comp.* **бли́же**) near, close, intimate
ближа́йший (*superl.*) nearest, next, neighbouring, immediate
бли́зко/бли́же (**от** + *G*) near/ er, close/r ((to) *sth.*)

блин (-á) pancake

блондин/-ка (*G pl.* **-нок**) a blond, fair(-haired) person (*male/ female*), (*f.*) a blonde

блу́зка (*G pl.* **-зок**) blouse

бобы́ (-о́в) beans

бог god

сла́ва бо́гу! thank god/ goodness!

бо́же мой! oh (my) god! good god/lord!

бога́тый (*comp.* **бога́че**) rich, wealthy

бок (**на боку́, на́ бок**; *pl.* **-á -о́в**) side (*of body or objects*)

бо́лее (*adv.*) more (*also used to form comp. adj. and adv. as Eng.* more, -er)

бо́лее или ме́нее more or less

боле́знь *f.* illness, disease

боле́льщик supporter, fan (*of team, etc.*)

боле́ть 1 (+ *I*) to be ill (with *sth.*), suffering (from *sth.*)
pf. **заболе́ть** to fall/be(come) ill

боле́ть 2 (*3rd pers. only,* **боли́т боля́т**) to hurt, ache

у меня́ боли́т голова́ I have a headache

у неё боле́ло го́рло she had a sore throat

боль *f.* pain, ache

больни́ца hospital

больно́й (**бо́лен больна́ -ы́**) ill, sore, sick, diseased

больно́й (-о́го)/больна́я (-о́й) (*as nn.*) patient, invalid (*male/ female*)

бо́льно it is painful, hurts

тебе́ бо́льно? does it hurt (you)? are you in pain?

(**бо́льше, бо́льший:** *see* **большо́й, мно́го**)

большинство́ majority, most (of)

большо́й (*no short form, but see* **вели́кий;** *comp.* **бо́льше, бо́льший;** *see also* **мно́го**) big, large, great (*esp. of physical size*)

бо́мба bomb

борода́ (бо́роду -ы́) beard

боро́ться (борю́сь бо́решься) to fight, struggle, strive, wrestle

борьба́ (за + *A*) struggle, fight (for *sth.*)

борщ (-á) borsch (*beetroot soup*)

боти́нки (-нок) (ankle-high) shoes, boots

боя́ться (бою́сь бои́шься; + *G*) to fear, be afraid (of)

брат (*pl.* **бра́тья -ьев**) brother

брать (беру́ берёшь; брала́)/ взять (возьму́ -мёшь; взяла́) to take, take hold of, get

брига́да brigade; team, crew (*of workers*)

брита́нский British

бри́тва razor, shaver

бри́ться/по- (бре́юсь бре́ешься) to shave (oneself), have a shave, get shaved

броса́ть/бро́сить (бро́шу -сишь) to throw, throw away

брю́ки (брюк) trousers, (*Amer.*) pants

брюне́т/-ка (*G pl.* **-ток**) a dark (-haired) person (*male/female*), (*f.*) a brunette

4

буди́льник alarm clock

буди́ть/раз- (**бужу́ бу́дишь**) to wake, wake up (*trans.*)

бу́дто *or* **как бу́дто** as if, as though

бу́дущий future, next (*as below*)

в бу́дущем году́ next year

на бу́дущей неде́ле next week

бу́дущее (-его) the future (*nn.*)

бу́ква letter (*of alphabet*)

бу́лочка (*G pl.* **-чек**) bun, roll (*of bread*)

бу́лочная (-ой) bread shop, baker's, bakery

бульва́р boulevard, avenue (*in city*)

бума́га paper (*material or document*)

бу́рный stormy, rough (*weather, sea*)

бу́ря storm (*caused by wind*)

бутербро́д (slice of) bread (*usu. and butter; with jam, meat, etc.*), canapé

бутербро́д с сы́ром bread and cheese

буты́лка (*G pl.* **-лок**) bottle

буфе́т sideboard; buffet, refreshment room/bar

бы (*or* **б** *after vowels*) (*particle used with past tense to form cond./subjunct.*)

быва́ть to be (*as a rule or often*); to happen, occur, take place

ле́том быва́ют гро́зы thunderstorms occur in summer, there are often storms in summer

бы́стро (*comp.* **быстре́е**) fast, quickly, rapidly

быть (*no pres. except* **есть**, *as below*; **был была́ бы́ло/и, не́ был(о/и) не была́**; *fut.* **бу́ду -ешь**; *imp.* **бу́дь(те)**) to be

есть (*neg.* **нет** + *G*) there is/are (not)

был, *etc.* (*neg.* **не́ было** + *G*) there was/were (not)

её не́ было/нет/не бу́дет she wasn't/isn't/won't be here

у меня́ (**есть/нет** + *G*), *etc.* I have/have not, *etc.*

у него́ есть/была́ сестра́ he has/had a sister

у нас нет вре́мени we haven't the time/have no time

бюро́ (*indecl.*) bureau, office (*esp. where one inquires*)

спра́вочное бюро́ information/inquiry office

бюро́ нахо́док lost-property office

в (**во** *before certain groups of consonants*) 1 (+ *A*) into, in; to; at (*a time*); on (*a day*); 2 (+ *P*) in, at (*a place*); in (*year, month*); 3 (+ *A*) a, per (*hour, etc.*)

она́ была́ в но́вой шля́пе she was wearing a new hat

ваго́н carriage, coach, car (*of train*)

ва́жный (-жен -жна́ -жны) important

ва́жно it is important

5

ва́за vase

валли́ец (-и́йца) Welsh(man) (*pl.* the Welsh)

валли́йка (*G pl.* **-и́ек**) Welsh(woman)

валли́йский Welsh (*adj.*)

валю́та currency, (*esp. convertible*) foreign/hard currency

ва́нна bath

    принима́ть/приня́ть ва́нну to have/take a bath

ва́нная (-ой) bathroom

варе́нье jam, preserve(s), marmalade

вари́ть/с- (варю́ ва́ришь) to boil, cook (*esp. by boiling*)

ваш* your; yours (*relates to* вы)

вверх up, upward(s) (*with motion*)

вверху́ above, overhead

    вверху́ страни́цы at the top of the page

вдоль (*+ G*) along, beside

    вдоль по (*+ D*) down, up (*river, street, etc.*)

вдруг suddenly, at once, all of a sudden

ведь you know, you see; isn't it? aren't they? *etc.*

ве́жливый polite

везде́ everywhere

(везти́: *see* **вози́ть)**

век (*pl.* **-а́ -о́в**) century; age (*era*)

вели́кий (-ка́ -ки́) great (*famous, grand*); (*used for* **большо́й** *in short forms*) big, large, *or* too big/large

Великобрита́ния Great Britain

велосипе́д bicycle, bike

    е́хать на велосипе́де to go by bicycle/bike, to cycle

верёвка string, cord; rope

ве́рить/по- (+ *D*/в + *A*) to believe, trust (*sb./sth.*)/to believe in (*sth.*)

    я тебе́ ве́рю I believe you

    я не ве́рю в бо́га I don't believe in god

ве́рно probably, likely, I suppose/imagine

(верну́ться: *see* **возвраща́ться)**

ве́рный (ве́рен верна́ ве́рны) true, faithful, loyal, sure; right, correct

вероя́тно probably, likely

верхо́м on horseback

    е́здить/е́хать верхо́м to ride (a horse), go riding

весёлый (ве́сел -а́ -ы) cheerful, merry, jolly

ве́село gaily

весе́нний spring (*adj.*)

весна́ spring (*season*)

    весно́й in (the) spring

(вести́: *see* **води́ть)**

весь/вся/всё/все* all, the whole

    всё (всего́) everything

    все (всех) everyone, everybody

    всего́ (хоро́шего) all the best! best wishes (and goodbye)

ве́тер (ве́тра, *but* **на ветру́)** wind

ве́тка (*G pl.* **ве́ток**) (*tree*) branch

ветчина́ ham

ве́чер (*pl.* **-а́ -о́в**) evening; (evening) party

    6, 7, ... 11 часо́в ве́чера 6, 7, ... 11 p.m.

ве́чером in the evening

вечери́нка (*G pl.* **-нок**) (evening) party

вече́рний evening (*adj.*); night (*adj.*; *of school*)

вещь *f.* (*pl.* **ве́щи веще́й**) thing

взгляд look (*that one gives*), glance, gaze, stare; view (*opinion*)

взгляну́ть *pf.* (**-ну́ -я́нешь**) (**на** + *A*) to cast a) glance, (throw a) look (at *sb./sth.*)

взро́слый (*adj. and nn.*) adult, grown-up

взрыв explosion

(**взять**: *see* **брать**)

вид look (*that sb./sth. has*), air, aspect, appearance; sight, view (*what is seen*); kind, sort, type, species

  у тебя́ хоро́ший вид you look nice/fine

  вид спо́рта (kind of) sport

вида́ть to see (*coll. for* **ви́деть**; *used esp. in neg. past tense*)

видеокассе́та video(cassette)

видеомагнитофо́н video(-recorder), VCR

ви́деть/у- (**ви́жу ви́дишь**) to see (*pf. generally has sense* to glimpse)

ви́деться/у- to see one another, meet

ви́дный (**-ден -дна́ -дны**) visible, to be seen

ви́дно one can see; apparently

ви́за visa, (official) stamp

ви́лка (*G pl.* **ви́лок**) fork

вино́ (*pl.* **ви́на**) wine

винова́тый guilty, to blame

винова́т(а)! sorry!

виногра́д grapes

висе́ть (**виси́т -я́т**) to hang, be (hanging)

витри́на (shop-)window

включа́ть/-чи́ть to include; to put/switch/turn on (*light, radio, etc.*)

включа́я (+ *A*) including

вкус taste

  име́ть хоро́ший вкус to taste nice

вку́сный (**-сен -сна́ -сны**) tasty, delicious, nice (*to eat*)

вме́сте (**с** + *I*) together (with)

вме́сто (+ *G*) instead of

  вме́сто того́, что́бы (+ *inf.*) instead of (*doing sth.*)

вниз down, downward(s), downstairs (*with motion*)

внизу́ down, downstairs (*position*)

  внизу́ страни́цы at the bottom/foot of the page

внима́ние attention, notice, consideration

внима́тельно attentively, carefully

(**вновь**: *see* **сно́ва**)

внук grandson (*pl. also* grandchildren)

вну́чка (*G pl.* **-чек**) granddaughter

во́время in/on time, at the right time

во́все не not at all

во-вторы́х secondly, in the second place

вода́ (**во́ду воды́**; *pl.* **во́ды**) water

води́тель *m.* driver (*private or*

professional, *e.g. in public transport*)

(**води́тельский**: *see* **пра́во**)

води́ть (**вожу́ во́дишь**) (*indef.*) to lead, take, bring (*sb. on foot*); to drive (*a vehicle*)

вести́/по- (**веду́ ведёшь; вёл вела́**) (*def.*) to lead, take, bring (*sb. on foot*); to drive (*a vehicle*); to lead (*of streets*)

вести́ себя́ to behave

во́дка vodka

вое́нный military, war (*adj.*)

возвраща́ться/возврати́ться (**-ащу́сь -ати́шься**) *and* **верну́ться** (**-у́сь -ёшься**) to go/come back, return

во́здух air (*the atmosphere*)

на (**откры́том**) **во́здухе** in the fresh air, outside, outdoors

возду́шный air (*adj.*)

вози́ть (**вожу́ во́зишь**) to carry, take (*with transport; indef.*)

везти́/по- (**везу́ везёшь; вёз везла́**) to carry, take (*with transport; def.*)

мне везёт/повезло́ I am/was lucky

во́зле (*adv., and prep.* + *G*) near, near by, close at hand

возмо́жно possibly; it is possible

возмо́жность *f.* possibility, opportunity, chance

во́зраст age (*period reached in life*)

война́ war

вокза́л (*use* **на**) (*large* railway/railroad) station

вокру́г (+ *G*) round, around (*in a circle*)

Во́лга the Volga

волейбо́л volleyball

волк (*pl.* **-и -о́в**) wolf

волна́ (*pl.* **во́лны волн волна́м**) wave (*of water, etc.*)

волнова́ться/вз- (**-ну́юсь -ну́ешься**) to worry, be(come) nervous/excited/upset

во́лосы (**воло́с -а́м**) hair (*of the head*)

вон out, away, off (*with motion*)

вон (**отсю́да**)! get out (of here)! clear off!

вон (**там**) there, over there

вообще́ in general, on the whole

во-пе́рвых first(ly), in the first place

вопро́с question; problem

вор (*pl.* **во́ры -о́в**) thief, robber

восемна́дцатый eighteenth

восемна́дцать eighteen

во́семь (**восьми́**) eight

во́семьдесят (**восьми́десяти**) eighty

восемьсо́т (**восьмисо́т -ста́м**) eight hundred

воскресе́нье Sunday

восто́к (*use* **на**) east

восто́чный east (*adj.*), eastern, easterly, oriental

восьмидеся́тый eightieth

восьмо́й eighth

вот here is/are, there is/are (*calling sth. to attention*)

вот где ... this is where ...

вот как ... that is how ...

впервы́е for the first time, first

вперёд forward(s) (*with motion*)

впереди́ in front

впечатле́ние impression

вполне́ fully, quite, entirely, perfectly

впро́чем (but) besides, (but) on the other hand, or rather

враг (-а́) enemy

врать/со- *or* **на- (вру врёшь; врала́)** to lie, tell a lie/lies (*vaguer than* **лгать**; *esp. common in 2nd person*)

врач (-а́) doctor, physician, medical practitioner

зубно́й врач dentist, dental surgeon

вре́мя *n.** time

вре́мя от вре́мени from time to time, now and then, occasionally

во вре́мя (+ *G*) during

тем вре́менем meanwhile

ско́лько вре́мени? how long?; what time is it?

времена́ го́да the seasons

(**всё, все**: *see* **весь**)

всегда́ always, ever

всё-таки all the same, still, even so, nevertheless

вско́ре soon, shortly (afterwards)

она́ вско́ре ушла́ she soon left/ left soon afterwards

вспомина́ть/вспо́мнить (*see also* **по́мнить**) to recall, remember, recollect

встава́ть (встаю́ -ёшь)/встать (вста́ну -ешь) to rise, get up, stand (up)

встре́ча meeting, encounter; reception, party, welcome

встреча́ть/встре́тить (-чу -тишь) to meet, encounter, receive, greet, welcome

встреча́ться, *etc.* to meet (each other)

всю́ду everywhere

вся́кий any; anyone, anybody

в тече́ние (+ *G*) during (the course of), throughout, over (the period of)

вто́рник (*use* **во**) Tuesday

второ́й second

второ́е (-о́го) *nn.* second course (*of meal*), main course/ dish

вуз (*i.e.* **вы́сшее уче́бное заведе́ние**) higher education(al) establishment (*university, college, institute, etc.*)

вулка́н volcano

вход entrance, entry, way in (*on foot*)

входи́ть (вхожу́ -о́дишь)/войти́ (войду́ -дёшь; вошёл -шла́) (**в** + *A*) to go/come/walk in, enter (*under own power*)

вчера́ yesterday

вчера́ у́тром yesterday morning

вчера́ ве́чером yesterday evening, last night

вы (вас вам ва́ми вас) you (*pl. and polite s.*)

выбира́ть/вы́брать (вы́беру -ешь) to choose, pick, select

вы́глядеть (-яжу -дишь) to look (*have the appearance of*)

хорошо́/пло́хо вы́глядеть to look well/ill

вызыва́ть/вы́звать (вы́зову -ешь) (+ *A*) to call (*sb.* out; for *sb.*/*sth. to come*; *sb. on the telephone*), send for (*doctor, etc.*), order (*taxi, etc.*)

выи́грывать/вы́играть to win, gain

выключа́ть/вы́ключить to put/ switch/turn off/out (*light, radio, etc.*)

вынима́ть/вы́нуть (-ну -нешь) (из + *G*) to take/pull (*sth.*) out (of *sth.*)

выполня́ть/вы́полнить to fulfil, perform, carry out, do (*duty, task, etc.*)

выраже́ние expression

высо́кий (высока́; *comp.* вы́ше, вы́сший) high, tall, big (*in height*)

высоко́ high, high up (*adv.*)

высота́ (*pl.* высо́ты) high place, height, altitude

вы́ставка (*use* на) exhibition, display, show

выступа́ть/вы́ступить (-плю -пишь) to appear (*make an appearance*), perform, sing, play, speak (*in public*)

вы́ход exit, way out

выходи́ть (-ожу́ -о́дишь)/вы́йти (вы́йду -дешь; вы́шел -шла) (из + *G*) to go/come/walk/ get out (of *sth.*), leave (*a place*) (*under own power*)

выходи́ть на (+ *A*) to look out on, give onto, face (*of windows, etc.*)

выходно́й день rest-day, day off, (day's) holiday

(вы́ше: *see* высо́кий)

вяза́ть/с-(вяжу́ вя́жешь) to knit

газ gas (*cf.* бензи́н)

газе́та (news)paper

газиро́ванная вода́ fizzy drink, soda (water)

га́зовый gas (*adj.*)

галере́я gallery

га́лстук (neck)tie, cravat, (*Pioneer's*) neckerchief

гара́ж (-а́) garage

гардеро́б wardrobe; cloakroom

гастроно́м delicatessen, (*Amer.*) deli

где where (*in what place*)

гекта́р hectare

геогра́фия geography

Герма́ния Germany

герои́ня heroine

геро́й hero

гимна́стика gymnastics, PT/ physical fitness exercises, drill

гита́ра guitar

глава́ (*pl.* гла́вы) chapter; chief, head

гла́вный main, chief, principal, head (*adj.*)

гла́дить/вы́- (гла́жу -дишь) to iron, press (*clothes*)

глаз (в глазу́; *pl.* глаза́ глаз -а́м) eye

гла́сность *f.* openness, plain speaking, publicity

глубо́кий (-ка́ -ки́; *comp.*
глу́бже) deep, profound
глубоко́ deep (*adv.*)
глу́пый (глупа́) foolish, silly,
stupid, daft
глухо́й (глу́х(и) -а́) deaf
гляде́ть/по- (**гляжу́ -ди́шь)** *and*
гля́нуть (гля́ну -нешь) (на +
A) to look, (*2nd pf.*) glance
(at *sth./sb.*)
гнездо́ nest
говори́ть/по- *and* **сказа́ть**
(**скажу́ ска́жешь)** to talk,
speak (*with 1st pf.*); to say, tell
(*with 2nd pf.*)
говоря́т, что it is said/people
say that
скажи́(те)! you don't say!
really!
так сказа́ть so to speak
как сказа́ть? how can I put it?
год (*pl.* **го́ды -о́в;** *see also* **ле́то**)
year
в про́шлом/э́том/бу́дущем
году́ last/this/next year
в 1934 (ты́сяча девятьсо́т
три́дцать четвёртом) году́
in 1934
Но́вый год New Year
с Но́вым го́дом! happy New
Year!
годовщи́на anniversary
голова́ (го́лову -ы́) head (*of*
body)
голо́дный (го́лоден -дна́ -дны)
hungry
го́лос (*pl.* **-а́ -о́в)** voice
голубо́й (sky/pale/light) blue
го́лый bare, naked

гора́ (го́ру -ы́; *pl.* **го́ры -а́м)**
mountain, (*high*) hill
идти́ в го́ру/по́д гору to go
uphill/downhill
гора́здо much, far (*with comp.*)
гора́здо лу́чше much/far better
го́рдый (горда́ -о -ы́) proud
го́ре grief, sorrow; trouble,
misfortune
горе́ть/с- (**гори́т -я́т)** to be alight/
on fire, burn; (*in pf.*) burn up/
out/down, be burnt down
го́рло throat
го́рничная (-ой) maid,
chambermaid
го́род (*pl.* **-а́ -о́в)** town, city
пое́здка за́ город a trip out of
town/to the country
жить за́ городом to live out of
town/in the suburbs
городско́й urban, municipal,
town, city (*adj.*)
горо́х (*no pl.*) peas
го́рький (го́рек горька́ го́рьки)
bitter
горя́чий (-ча́ -чи́) hot (*esp. to the*
touch or taste)
господи́н (*pl.* **господа́)**
gentleman; Mr (*pl.* Messrs)
господа́! (ladies and)
gentlemen!
госпожа́ lady; Mrs, Miss, Ms
(*These two words are used of*
visitors from non-Communist
countries)
гости́ная (-ой) sitting-room,
drawing-room, lounge
гости́ница hotel, inn
гость *m.* (*pl.* **-и -е́й)** guest, visitor

11

идти́ в го́сти (к + *D*) to visit (*sb. at his or her place*)

быть в гостя́х (у + *G*) to be visiting/on a visit to (*sb. at his or her place*)

госуда́рственный State (*adj.*), public (*of the State*), national

госуда́рство State, nation, country (*sovereign entity*)

гото́вить/при- *and* **под-** (**-влю -вишь**) (*with 1st pf.*) to prepare, get ready, cook, make (*meal*), learn, do (*homework, etc.*); (*with 2nd pf.*) to prepare, train (*pupils for an examination, etc.*)

гото́виться, *etc.* (к + *D*) to prepare (oneself), get ready (*for an examination, etc.*)

гото́вый ready, prepared, willing

гра́дус degree (*measurement*)

два́дцать пять гра́дусов Це́льсия (*or* **по Це́льсию**; *written* 25°) twenty-five degrees Celsius/centigrade (25° C)

граждани́н (*pl.* **гра́ждане -дан**)/ **гражда́нка** (*G pl.* **-нок**) citizen (*male/female*; *used also to attract attention* – I say, excuse me, hey (you), *etc.*)

грамм (*G pl.* **грамм** *in speech, otherwise* **-ов**) gram(me)

грани́ца boundary, limit, frontier, border

уе́хать за грани́цу to go abroad

жить за грани́цей to live abroad

гре́ческий Greek (*adj.*)

гриб (**-а́**) mushroom

грипп influenza, (the) flu

гроза́ (*pl.* **гро́зы**) (thunder)storm

гром thunder

гром греми́т (*from* **греме́ть**) it is thundering

грома́дный (**-ден -дна**) immense, colossal, huge, vast, enormous

гро́мкий (*comp.* **гро́мче**) loud

гро́мко loud(ly), aloud

гру́бый (**груба́**) rough, coarse, harsh, rude, crude

грузови́к (**-а́**) lorry, truck

гру́ппа group

гру́стный (**-тен -тна́ -тны**) sad, sorrowful, melancholy

мне гру́стно I am/feel sad

гру́ша pear

гря́зный (**-зен -зна́ -зны**) dirty, filthy, muddy

губа́ (*pl.* **гу́бы -а́м**) lip

гуля́ть/по- to walk, have/go for a walk

ГУМ (**госуда́рственный универса́льный магази́н**) GUM, State department store

густо́й (**гу́ст -а́ -ы**; *comp.* **гу́ще**) thick, dense (*of hair, forest, fog, etc.*)

да yes; that's right, no (*when agreeing with a negative used in a question*)

Она́ не англича́нка? She's not English?

Да, не англича́нка. No, she isn't (English).

cf. **Нет, (она́) англича́нка.**
Yes, she is (English).
дава́ть (даю́ даёшь; *imp.*
**дава́й(те))/дать (дам дашь
даст дади́м дади́те даду́т;**
imp. **да́й(те); дала́)** (+ *A* +
D; + *D* + *inf.*) to give (*sth. to
sb.*); to let (*sb. know, etc.*)
дава́й(те) (+ *inf. or fut. 1st pers.
pl.*) let's (*do sth.*)
дава́йте петь! let's sing
дава́й ся́дем! let's sit down
давно́ long ago/since; for a long
time (*up till now*)
**я давно́ не ви́дела твоего́
бра́та** I haven't seen your
brother for a long time
вы давно́ здесь? have you been
here long?.
да́же even
да́же не not even
(да́лее: *see* **и т. д.)**
далеко́ (*comp.* **да́льше)** (**от** + *G*)
far (from), a long way (from)
чита́йте да́льше read on/
further
да́мский ladies'
да́нный given, present (*time or
matter in question*)
дари́ть/по- (**дарю́ да́ришь)** to
give (*as a present*)
(дать: *see* **дава́ть)**
да́ча (*use* **на)** dacha (*Russian
holiday or weekend home
outside the city of residence*)
уе́хать на да́чу to leave for the
country
отдыха́ть на да́че to be
holidaying in the country

два *m. and n.*/**две** *f.* (**двух двум
двумя́ двух)** two
двадца́тый twentieth
два́дцать (-ти́) twenty
двена́дцатый twelfth
двена́дцать twelve
дверь *f.* (*pl.* **-и -е́й)** door
две́сти (двухсо́т двумста́м, *etc.*)
two hundred
**дви́гаться/дви́нуться (-нусь
-нешься)** to move, start
(moving), get going
движе́ние movement; traffic
(*movement of vehicles*)
дво́е (двои́х, *etc., but usu.* replaced
by **двух,** *etc.*) two (*used esp.
where G pl. is lexically
obligatory*)
дво́е су́ток 48 hours, two days
(and nights)
нас дво́е there are two of us
дво́йка (*G pl.* **дво́ек)** a two, bad/
poor mark, D (*in Soviet 5-
point marking system*)
двор (-а́) yard, courtyard,
playground
на дворе́ outside, outdoors,
out-of-doors
дворе́ц (дворца́) palace
двою́родная сестра́ (first) cousin
(*female*)
двою́родный брат (first) cousin
(*male*)
де́вочка (*G pl.* **-чек)** (little) girl
(*before maturity*)
де́вушка (*G pl.* **-шек)** girl (*after
maturity*), young woman;
waitress (*used when trying to
catch the attention of one*)

девяно́сто (*GDIP* **-о́ста**) ninety

девяно́стый ninetieth

девятна́дцатый nineteenth

девятна́дцать nineteen

девя́тый ninth

де́вять (**-ти́**) nine

девятьсо́т (**девятисо́т -ста́м**) nine hundred

дед *or* **де́душка** (*G pl.* **-шек**) *m.* grandfather, granddad, grandpa

дежу́рный duty (*adj.*), on duty; (*as nn., m. or f.*) duty person

дежу́рная по общежи́тию the woman (on duty) at the hostel

де́йствие effect, action; operation, functioning; act (*of play*)

действи́тельный (**-лен -льна**) real, actual, true, authentic

де́йствовать (**-ствую -ешь**) to act, operate, function, work; to have an effect, take effect

дека́брь *m.* (**-бря́**) December

де́лать/с- to do; to make

де́латься/с- to become, get, grow

де́ло (*pl.* **дела́**) affair, matter, business

по дела́м on business

как дела́? how are things (with you)? how are you (doing)?

в/на са́мом де́ле in fact, in reality, actually, indeed, really

в чём де́ло? what's the matter/up?

де́ло в том, что . . . the fact/point/question is that . . .

день *m.* (**дня**) day

днём in the daytime, (*esp.*) in the afternoon

до́брый день good afternoon/day (*in greeting*)

час/2, 3, 4 часа́/5 часо́в дня 1, 2, 3, 4, 5 p.m.

день рожде́ния birthday

(поздравля́ю тебя́) с днём рожде́ния! happy birthday/many happy returns (of the day)

де́ньги (**де́нег деньга́м**) money, cash

дере́вня (*G pl.* **-ве́нь**) village (*smaller than* **село́**); the country(side)

де́рево (*pl.* **дере́вья -вьев**) tree; wood (*material; s. only*)

деревя́нный wooden, wood (*adj.*)

держа́ть (**-жу́ де́ржишь**) to hold, hold on to, keep (hold of)

деся́тый tenth

де́сять (**-ти́**) ten

(**де́ти**: *see* **ребёнок**)

де́тский child's, children's

де́тский сад *or* **детса́д** nursery school, kindergarten

де́тство childhood

дешёвый (*comp.* **деше́вле**) cheap, good value

дёшево cheap(ly); it is cheap

джи́нсы (**-ов**) jeans

дива́н divan, sofa, couch, settee

ди́кий wild, savage

дипло́м diploma, degree

дире́ктор (*pl.* **-а́ -о́в**) director, head, manager, principal

дире́ктор шко́лы headmaster/mistress

14

дискотéка discothèque, disco

длинá length

длинóй в шесть мéтров *or* **шесть мéтров в длинý** six metres long/in length

дли́нный (-нен -ннá -нны) long (*esp. of measurement*)

для (+ *G*) for (*intended for, in relation to*)

дневни́к (-á) diary, journal, record (*of trip, etc.*), homework and mark book (*in school*)

вести́ дневни́к to keep a diary (**днём:** *see* **день**)

до (+ *G*) as far as, (up) to (*place*); (up) till, until, before (*time*)

до понедéльника till Monday, I'll see you (on) Monday

добавля́ть/добáвить (-влю -вишь) to add

дóбрый (добрá -ы́) kind

дóброе ýтро, *etc.* good morning, *etc.*

добрó пожáловать! welcome!

бýдьте добры́ (+ *inf.*) be so kind (as to *do sth.*), could you please (*do sth.*), would you mind (*doing sth.*)?

довóльно rather, quite, fairly, enough, pretty (*adv.*)

довóльный (-лен -льна; + *I*) satisfied, content(ed), pleased (with *sth./sb.*)

доезжáть/доéхать (доéду -дешь; **до** + *G*) to reach, arrive (at), go (as far as), get (to) (*with transport*)

дождли́вый rainy

дождь *m.* (дождя́) rain

дождь идёт *or* **идёт дождь** it is raining

шёл дождь it was raining

доклáд (**о** + *P*) report, address, paper, talk (on/about *sth.*)

дóктор (*pl.* -á -óв) doctor

докумéнты (-ов) documents, papers (*for travel, etc.*)

дóлго (*comp.* **дóльше**) (for) a long time, long (*during a period seen as a whole*)

он дóлго говори́л по телефóну he spoke for a long time on the phone

дóлжен -жнá -жны́ must, have to, ought to, should; owe

онá должнá (былá) рабóтать she has (had) to work

онá должнá (былá) мне пять рублéй she owes (owed) me five roubles

он, должнó быть, ушёл he must have gone

доли́на valley

дóллар dollar

дом (*pl.* -á -óв) house, home, building, tower-block, block of flats

дом óтдыха rest home, holiday centre

в дом/дóме inside (the house), indoors (*motion/position*)

дóма (at) home, in

не дóма not (at) home, out

домáшний domestic, house, home (*adj.*)

домóй home (*to one's home*)

домохозя́йка (*G pl.* -я́ек) housewife

Дон (на Дону́) the Don (*river and region*)

доро́га road, way, journey

по доро́ге on the way

дорого́й (*comp.* **доро́же**) dear, expensive

до́рого dearly, dear (*adv.*)

доро́жка (*G pl.* **-жек**) path, lane, track; runway

(**доро́жный:** *see* **чек**)

доса́дно it is annoying/a nuisance

(**до свида́ния:** *see* **свида́ние**)

доска́ (**до́ску доски́**) board

(**кла́ссная**) **доска́** blackboard

доска́ почёта board/roll of honour

достава́ть (**достаю́ -ёшь**)/ **доста́ть** (**доста́ну -ешь**) to get, take, obtain, fetch

доста́точно enough, sufficiently

достопримеча́тельности (**-ей**) the sights (*of a town, etc.*)

доходи́ть (**-ожу́ -о́дишь**)/**дойти́** (**дойду́ -дёшь; дошёл дошла́**) (**до** + *G*) to reach, arrive (at), go/walk (as far as), get (to) (*under own power*)

дочь* *f.* daughter

друг (*pl.* **друзья́ -зе́й -зья́м**) friend

друг дру́га each other, one another

друг с дру́гом with each other, etc.

друго́й other, another (*adj. and pron.*); different (*not the same*)

что́-то друго́е something else

на друго́й день (on) the next day

дру́жба friendship

дуб (*pl.* **-ы́ -о́в**) oak(-tree)

ду́мать/по- to think

ду́ра fool (*female*)

дура́к (**-а́**) fool (*male*)

дуть/по- (**ду́ет**) to blow (*of wind*); to be draughty

духи́ (**-о́в**) perfume, scent

душ shower(-bath)

принима́ть(приня́ть) душ to have/take a shower

душа́ (**ду́шу души́**) soul, heart

от (всей) души́ with all one's heart

ду́шно it is stuffy/close/sultry

дым smoke

ды́ня melon

дя́дя *m.* uncle

Евро́па Europe

европе́йский European (*adj.*)

его́ his; its

еда́ food

за едо́й while eating, over a meal

едва́ hardly, scarcely, (only) just

едва́ не almost, nearly, all but

едини́ца a one, bottom/very bad/ poor mark, E (*in Soviet 5-point marking system; practically never awarded*)

еди́нственный only, one and only, sole

её her, hers; its

е́здить (**е́зжу е́здишь**) (*indef.*) to go, come, ride, drive, travel (*not on foot*)

е́хать/по- (**е́ду е́дешь**: *imp.*
поезжа́й(те)) *for both aspects,*
neg. **не е́зди(те)**) (*def.*) to go,
come, ride, drive, travel (*not*
on foot)
ёлка (*G pl.* **ёлок**) fir(-tree);
Christmas tree, New Year tree
е́сли if
  е́сли не if not, unless
  е́сли . . ., то . . . if . . ., then . . .
(**есть** 1: *see* **быть**)
есть 2 (**ем ешь ест еди́м -и́те -я́т**;
  ел е́ла; *impf.* **ешь(те)**) to eat
  pf. **съесть,** *etc.* to eat (up)
  pf. **пое́сть,** *etc.* to have
  something to eat/a bite (to eat)
(**е́хать**: *see* **е́здить**)
ещё *or* **всё ещё** still
  ещё не(т) not yet
  ещё раз (once) again/more
  ещё оди́н another (one), one
  more
  ещё хле́ба some more bread
  что ещё? what else?

жаке́т (*woman's*) jacket
жале́ть/по- to pity, be sorry for
жа́лко *or* **жаль** it is a pity/shame
  как жаль! what a pity/shame!
  мне жа́лко их I'm sorry for
  them
жара́ hot weather, heat(wave)
жа́реный fried, roast, grilled
жа́рить/из- to fry, roast, grill,
  cook (*in these senses*)
жа́ркий (*compr.* **жа́рче**) hot (*esp.*
  of weather)
  жа́рко it is hot
  нам жа́рко we're hot

жарко́е (**-о́го**) roast (meat)
жда́ть/подо- (**жду ждёшь**;
  ждала́) to wait, wait for; to
  expect
  подожди́(те)! wait! hold on!
же (*emphatic particle, as below*;
  see also **тот**)
  сейча́с же immediately, at once
  что́ же мне де́лать? what *shall*
  I do?
жела́ние (**+** *G*) wish, desire (for
  sth.)
жела́ть/по- to wish, want, desire
  жела́ю тебе́ успе́ха I wish you
  success/good luck!
желе́зная доро́га railway,
  (*Amer.*) railroad
  по желе́зной доро́ге by rail/
  train
желе́зный iron (*adj.*)
жёлтый yellow
жена́ wife
жена́тый married (*of man or a*
  couple)
жени́ться *impf. and pf.* (**женю́сь**
  же́нишься) (**на +** *P*) to
  marry, get married (to) (*of man*
  or a couple)
же́нский woman's, women's, girl's,
  girls', female, feminine
же́нщина woman
жесто́кий (**жестока́**) cruel,
  brutal, harsh
живо́й (**жив жива́ жи́вы**) alive;
  living; lively
живо́т (**-а́**) belly, stomach
живо́тное (**-ого**) *nn.* animal
жизнь *f.* life
жи́тель *m.* inhabitant, resident

17

жить (живу́ живёшь; жила́) to
  live
журна́л magazine, journal,
  periodical

за (+ *A or I*; *see also* что) 1 (*A
  motion/I position*) behind,
  beyond, the other side of,
  across, over; to/at (*table,
  piano, meal, etc.*); 2 (*A*) for
  (*exchange, on behalf,
  purpose*); by (*of taking by the
  hand, etc.*); 3 (*I*) for (*idea of
  fetching*); after (*following in
  sequence*)
заба́вный (-вен -вна) amusing,
  funny
забыва́ть/забы́ть (забу́ду -ешь)
  to forget; to leave (behind;
  unintentionally)
(заведе́ние: *see* вуз)
зави́сеть (-сит) (от + *G*) to
  depend (on *sb./sth.*)
заво́д (*use* на) factory, works, mill,
  plant
за́втра tomorrow
  до за́втра! till tomorrow/see
   you tomorrow
  за́втра у́тром, *etc.* tomorrow
   morning, *etc.*
  за́втра ве́чером tomorrow
   evening/night
за́втрак breakfast
  (второ́й) за́втрак (*light*) lunch
за́втракать/по- to (have)
  breakfast/(*light or early*) lunch
(за грани́цу/-ей: *see* грани́ца)
загрязне́ние pollution

задава́ть/зада́ть вопро́с (+ *D*)
  (за + дава́ть/да́ть, *but* за́дал
  -а́ -и) to ask/put a question
  (to *sb.*)
зада́ние task, job, assignment
  дома́шнее зада́ние homework
  (assignment)
зада́ча problem (*to be solved*)
заезжа́ть/зае́хать (зае́ду -дешь)
  (к + *D or* в/на + *A*; за + *I*)
  to call, drop/look in (on *sb.*/at
  a place*; *with transport*); to call
  for, go to get, fetch, collect
  (*sth.*; *with transport*)
зажига́ть/заже́чь (зажгу́
  зажжёшь -гу́т; зажёг
  -жгла́) to light, set fire to; to
  strike (*a match*)
зака́зывать/заказа́ть (закажу́
  -а́жешь) to order (*meal, etc.*);
  to book, reserve (*tickets, etc.*)
зака́нчивать/зако́нчить to
  complete, conclude, finish
  (off), wind up, end (*trans.*)
зако́н law
закрыва́ть/закры́ть (закро́ю
  -ешь) to close, shut (*trans.*);
  to turn off (*tap*)
  закрыва́ться, *etc.* to close, shut
  (*intrans.*), be closed/shut
закры́тый closed, shut
заку́ска (*often pl.*; *G pl.* -сок)
  hors d'œuvre, appetizer, snack
зал hall
  зал ожида́ния waiting-room
замерза́ть/замёрзнуть
  (замёрзнет -нут; замёрз
  -ла) to freeze, be freezing, (*in
  pf.*) be frozen

замеча́тельный (-лен -льна) remarkable, wonderful

замеча́ть/заме́тить (-чу -тишь) to notice, take notice/note (of), observe, remark

заме́ть(те) notice, *etc.*; mind you

замо́к (замка́) lock

закры́ть дверь на замо́к to lock the door

за́муж(ем) (*as below*)

вы́йти за́муж (за + *A*) to marry (*sb.*), get married (*to sb.*; *of woman marrying a man*)

она́ за́мужем (за + *I*) she is married (to *sb.*)

занима́ться (+ *I*) to study, do, go in for (*subject, sport, etc.*); to be studying, be busy/engaged/occupied (with/in/by)

заня́тия *n. pl.* **(-ий)** (*use* на) studies, work, lessons

за́нятый (-ят -ята́ -яты) busy, occupied, engaged, (*of seat*) taken

за́пад (*use* на) west

за́падный west (*adj.*), western, westerly, occidental

за́пах smell, odour

запи́ска (*G pl.* -сок) note (*sth. written, often pl.*)

запи́сывать/записа́ть (-ишу́ -и́шешь) to write down, note, make/take notes on (*lecture, etc.*); to record (*sound*)

заполня́ть/запо́лнить to fill up/out/in (*form, etc.*)

зараба́тывать/зарабо́тать to earn (*money*)

зарпла́та pay, wages, salary

заслу́живать/заслужи́ть (-ужу́ -у́жишь) to deserve, merit, be worthy of; to earn, win, gain (*reward, etc.*)

заставля́ть/заста́вить (-влю -вишь) to make, force, compel (*sb.* (*to*) *do sth.*)

засыпа́ть/засну́ть (-ну́ -нёшь) to fall asleep, go (off) to sleep

зате́м then, after that, next

зато́ but then, on the other hand, there again, however

заходи́ть (-ожу́ -о́дишь)/зайти́ (зайду́ -ёшь; зашёл -шла́) (к + *D or* в/на + *A*; за + *I*) to call, drop/look in (on *sb.* / at *a place*; *on foot*); to call for, go to get, fetch, collect (*sth.*; *on foot*)

заче́м what for, why

защища́ть/защити́ть (-ищу́ -ити́шь) to defend, protect, guard

звать/по- (зову́ -ёшь; звала́) to call (*sb. to come*; *for help, etc.*)

как тебя́ зову́т? what is your name/are you called?

меня́ зову́т Ната́ша my name is Natasha

меня́ зову́т Ната́шей they call me Natasha

звезда́ (*pl.* звёзды) star

зверь *m.* (*pl.* -и -е́й) wild animal, beast

звони́ть/за- to ring (*of telephone, bell*)

звони́ть/по- (по телефо́ну) (+ D + в/на + A) to ring (up), (tele)phone, (*Amer.*) call (*sb. at a place*)
 она́ позвони́ла мне в кварти́ру/на рабо́ту she rang me at the flat/at work
звоно́к (звонка́) bell (*door bell, school bell, etc.*)
 звоно́к по телефо́ну phone call
звук sound
зда́ние building
здесь here (*in this place*)
здоро́вый healthy, well
 будь здоро́в(а)/бу́дьте здоро́вы! cheers! 'bye! good luck! take care! (God) bless (you)! ciao! look after yourself!
 здоро́во! hi! hallo!
 (как) здоро́во! good for/on you! nice one! jolly good! super! great! neat!
здоро́вье health
 за (ва́ше) здоро́вье! here's to you! your health! cheers! (*when drinking*)
 как ва́ше здоро́вье? how are you (keeping)?
здра́вствуй(те)! hallo! hi! good morning, *etc.*, how do you do?
зелёный green
землетрясе́ние earthquake
земля́ (зе́млю земли́) earth, land, ground
зе́ркало mirror, looking-glass
 смотре́ть(ся) в зе́ркало to look (at oneself) in the mirror

зима́ (зи́му зимы́) winter
 зимо́й in (the) winter
зи́мний winter (*adj.*)
злой (зол зла) wicked, vicious, bad, evil, (*of animals*) savage, fierce; (*in short forms*) angry, cross, mad
змея́ (*pl.* зме́и змей) snake
знак sign, mark, symbol, signal
 мя́гкий знак (ь) (Russian) soft sign
 твёрдый знак (ъ) (Russian) hard sign
знако́миться/по- (-млюсь -мишься) (с + I) to make (the) acquaintance (with/of), become acquainted (with), get to know (*sb./sth.*), introduce oneself (to *sb.*)
 (по)знако́мьтесь! let me introduce you; meet (*sb. introduced*)
знако́мый acquainted, familiar; (*as nn.*) acquaintance, someone I/you know, friend
знамени́тый famous, celebrated
зна́мя *n.* * banner, standard, flag (*esp. one with slogan*)
зна́ние knowledge
знать to know
 не знать not to know, to be unaware/ignorant of
значе́ние meaning, sense, significance; importance
 э́то не име́ет значе́ния that/it doesn't matter
зна́чить (зна́чит) to mean
 что э́то зна́чит? what does this/it mean?

20

Vocabulary

значо́к (значка́) badge

(зову́т: *see* **звать)**

золото́й golden, gold (*adj.*)

зо́нтик umbrella; sunshade

зоопа́рк zoo, zoological gardens

(зре́лость *f.*: *see* **аттеста́т)**

зри́тель *m.* spectator, observer, member of the audience (*at a spectacle*)

зуб (*pl.* **зу́бы -о́в**) tooth

зубно́й dental, tooth (*adj.*)

  зубна́я па́ста toothpaste

  зубна́я щётка toothbrush

и and

  и … и … both … and …

игра́ (*pl.* **и́гры**) game

  олимпи́йские и́гры Olympic games, Olympics

игра́ть (в + *A* / **на** + *P*) to play (*game/instrument*)

игру́шка (*G pl.* **-шек**) toy

иде́я idea

(идти́: *see* **ходи́ть)**

из (изо *before certain groups of consonants*; + *G*) out of, from; (made) of

  оди́н из вас one of you

  из де́рева (made) of wood, wooden

изба́ (*pl.* **и́збы**) izba (*wooden house or hut*)

изве́стный (-тен -тна) well-known, famous

  как вам изве́стно as you know/are well aware

извиня́ть/-ни́ть to excuse, pardon

  извини́(те) (меня́)! (I'm) sorry!

извиня́юсь (I'm) sorry, I apologise

из-за (+ *G*) from behind; up from (*table, etc.*); because of

изменя́ть/-ни́ть (-ю́ -е́нишь) to change, alter (*make different*)

изменя́ться, *etc.* to change, alter (*become different*)

изуча́ть/-чи́ть (-чу́ -у́чишь) to learn, study (*sth.*)

икра́ caviar (*salted roe of sturgeon*)

и́ли or

  и́ли … и́ли … either … or …

и́менно precisely, just, exactly, to be exact

име́ть to have (*esp. of abstract things*)

  име́ть значе́ние to be of importance

  име́ть ме́сто to take place

  име́ть в виду́ to have in mind, mean; to intend, plan; to bear/ keep in mind, not to forget

и́мя *n.** name (*esp. given name*)

и́мя-о́тчество (first) name and patronymic

  Библиоте́ка и́мени Ле́нина the Lenin Library

ина́че differently, in a different way; otherwise, or else

Инди́йский океа́н the Indian Ocean

И́ндия India

инжене́р engineer (*sb. with higher technical qualifications*)

иногда́ sometimes, now and then

иностра́нец (-а́нца)/-а́нка (*G. pl.* **-нок**) foreigner (*male/female*)

21

иностра́нный foreign

институ́т institute, college (*of specialized higher education*)

инструме́нт tool, instrument (*incl. musical*)

интере́с interest

интере́сный (-сен -сна) interesting

интере́сно (знать), ... it would be interesting to know ... I wonder ...

интересова́ть/за- (-су́ет) to interest

интересова́ться, *etc.* (*+ I*) to be (*pf.* become) interested (in *sth.*)

её интересу́ет му́зыка *or* **она́ интересу́ется му́зыкой** she is interested in music

Интури́ст Intourist (*Soviet state tourist agency*)

ирла́ндец (-дца) Irish(man) (*pl.* the Irish)

ирла́ндка (*G pl.* -**док**) Irish(woman)

Ирла́ндия Ireland

ирла́ндский Irish (*adj.*)

иска́ть/по- (ищу́ и́щешь) to look/search for, seek

и́скренний sincere, frank, candid

иску́сство art

испа́нец (-а́нца) Spaniard, Spanish (*male*; *pl.* the Spanish)

испа́нка (*G pl.* -**нок**) Spaniard, Spanish (*female*)

Испа́ния Spain

испа́нский Spanish (*adj.*)

исправля́ть/испра́вить (-влю -вишь) to correct, put right, rectify

испыта́ние trial, test (*e.g. of weapon*)

исто́рия history; story (*narrative*)

исчеза́ть/исче́знуть (-ну -нешь; исче́з -ла) to disappear, vanish

ита́к (and) so, thus

Ита́лия Italy

италья́нец (-я́нца) Italian (*male*)

италья́нка (*G pl.* -**нок**) Italian (*female*)

италья́нский Italian (*adj.*)

и т. д. (и так да́лее) and so on, etc.

их their; theirs

ию́ль *m.* July

ию́нь *m.* June

к (ко *before certain groups of consonants*; *+ D*) to, up to, towards; by (*a time*); for (*with intention, etc.*)

к врачу́ to the doctor's

к понеде́льнику by Monday

к чему́? what for?

кабине́т study; private office; surgery, consulting-room; room (*for specialized purposes, e.g. in school*)

лингафо́нный кабине́т language laboratory

Кавка́з (*use* **на**) the Caucasus

ка́ждый each, every; everyone

каза́ться/по- (ка́жется) to seem, appear, look

ка́жется/(по)каза́лось it

22

seems/seemed, *etc.*, apparently, evidently

он ка́жется больны́м he looks ill

он, ка́жется, бо́лен he's ill, apparently

как how; as, like; what? (*as below*; *see also* **бу́дто**)

как по-ру́сски 'caviar'? what is the Russian for 'caviar'?

како́й which, what, what sort/kind of?

календа́рь *m.* (**-аря́**) calendar

калькуля́тор *or* **микрокалькуля́тор** (pocket) calculator

ка́мень *m.* (**ка́мня**; *pl.* **ка́мни -не́й**) stone, rock

ка́мера хране́ния (багажа́) cloakroom, left-luggage office, (*Amer.*) checkroom

ками́н fireplace, open fire, fireside

Кана́да Canada

кана́дец (-а́дца) Canadian (*male*)

кана́дка (*G pl.* **-док**) Canadian (*female*)

кана́дский Canadian (*adj.*)

кани́кулы (-кул; *use* **на)** holidays, vacation (*break between academic terms*)

капита́н captain

капу́ста cabbage

каранда́ш (-а́) pencil

ка́рий brown (*of eyes*)

карма́н pocket

карма́нные де́ньги pocket money

ка́рта map; (*in pl.*) (playing-)cards

карти́на picture (*large*), painting

карти́нка (*G pl.* **-нок**) picture (*small*), illustration

карто́фель (*no pl.*) *m. or* **карто́шка** (*no. pl.*) potatoes

каса́ться/косну́ться (-ну́сь -нёшься) (**+ *G*)** to touch; to touch (up)on; to concern, relate to (*sth./sb.*)

э́то тебя́ не каса́ется that doesn't concern you/has nothing to do with you/is none of your business

что каса́ется (**+ *G*)** with regard to, as regards, as to (*sth./sb.*)

Каспи́йское мо́ре the Caspian Sea

ка́сса cash-desk, check-out (counter/desk); box-office, booking-office, ticket window

кассе́та cassette(-tape)

касси́р/-ша cashier, check-out operator; box-office/booking clerk (*male/female*)

кастрю́ля saucepan

ката́ться/по- to ride, have/go for a ride

ката́ться на велосипе́де to go cycling/for bike rides

ката́ться на ло́дке to go boating

ката́ться на лы́жах to go skiing

ката́ться на конька́х/ро́ликах to go (ice/roller-)skating

ката́ться на са́нках to go tobogganing

ката́ться на ло́шади/верхо́м to go (horse-)riding

като́к (катка́) (ice)rink, skating-rink

кафе́ *n. indecl.* café, coffee-shop/-house

ка́чество quality

ка́ша (*Russian varieties of*) porridge, gruel, (semolina/rice) pudding

ка́шель *m.* (**ка́шля**) cough

ка́шлять to cough, have a cough

квадра́тный square (*adj.*)

кварти́ра flat, apartment

квас kvas (*fermented Russian drink from rye, bread, etc.*)

ке́мпинг camping ground/area, camp(ing) site

кефи́р kefir (*fermented Russian milk drink resembling liquid yoghurt*)

Ки́ев Kiev

килогра́мм (*G pl.* **килогра́мм** *in speech, otherwise* **-ов**) *or* **кило́** *n. indecl.* kilogram, kilo

киломе́тр kilometre

кино́ *n. indecl.* cinema (*place and art*), (motion) pictures, movies

кинотеа́тр cinema (*place*), movie theatre

кио́ск kiosk, news-stand

кирпи́ч (-а́) brick; bricks

кисе́ль *m.* kissel (*Russian stewed-fruit dessert, resembling blancmange*)

ки́слый sour, acid

кита́ец (-а́йца) Chinaman, Chinese (*male*; *pl.* the Chinese)

китая́нка (*G pl.* **-нок**) Chinese (*female*)

Кита́й China

кита́йский Chinese (*adj.*)

класс class, grade, form, standard; classroom

кла́ссный class (*adj.*; *pertaining to the class or classroom*)

класть (кладу́ -дёшь; клал)/ положи́ть (-жу́ -о́жишь) to lay, put, put down, place (*sth. in a lying position*)

кле́тка (*G pl.* **-ток**) cage

кли́мат climate

клуб club

ключ (ключа́) key

ключ от кварти́ры key to the flat, flat key

кни́га book

кни́жка (*G pl.* **-жек**) book (*esp. small, or for children*); notebook, pocket-book, bankbook, cheque-book, *etc.*

кни́жный book (*adj.*)

кни́жный магази́н bookshop

кни́жный шкаф bookcase (*with doors*)

ковёр (ковра́) carpet, rug

когда́ when

ко́жа skin; leather

коза́ (*pl.* **ко́зы**) goat, she-goat, nanny goat

козёл (козла́) (he-)goat, billy goat

колбаса́ sausage (*salami or other sliceable varieties*)

колго́тки (-ток) (pair of) tights, (*Amer.*) pantihose

колеба́ться/по- (коле́блюсь -лешься) to hesitate, waver, vacillate

коле́но (*pl.* **коле́ни -ей**) knee

Vocabulary

колесо (*pl.* **колёса**) wheel
количество quantity, amount
коллектив collective, group, body, association
колокол (*pl.* **-а -ов**) bell (*of church, etc.*)
колхоз (collective) farm
колхозник/-ница (collective) farmer, farmworker (*male/ female*)
кольцо (*pl.* **кольца колец**) ring
команда team; crew
командир commanding officer, comander; captain (*of ship*)
комитет committee, board
коммунизм communism
коммунист communist
коммунистический communist (*adj.*)
комната room
комод chest of drawers, bureau
компакт-диск compact disc
композитор composer
компот stewed fruit, compote, (fruit) sauce
компьютер computer (*personal, etc.*)
комсомол Komsomol, League of Young Communists
комсомолец (-льца)/комсомолка (*G pl.* **-лок**) member of the Komsomol (*male/female*)
комсомольский Komsomol (*adj.*)
конверт envelope
кондуктор (*pl.* **-а -ов**)/**-ша** conductor(-tress), guard (*on public transport*)
конец (конца) end
в конце сада/улицы at the

end/bottom of the garden/ street
в конце концов in the end, after all, eventually
конечно of course, naturally, certainly, sure(ly), sure enough
консервы (**-ов**) tinned/canned goods (*meat, fish, fruit, vegetables*), bottled/pickled fruit/vegetables
контора office (*where one works*)
контролёр ticket-inspector/- collector
конфета sweet, (*Amer.*) candy
шоколадные конфеты chocolates
концерт (*use* **на**) concert, recital (*of music*)
концертный зал concert hall
кончать/кончить (+ *A/impf. inf.*) to finish, end (*sth./doing sth.*)
кончаться, *etc.* to (come to an) end, finish (*intrans.; pf. also* to be finished/over)
коньки (**-ов**) (ice-)skates
коньяк (**-а**) brandy, cognac
копейка (*G pl.* **копеек**) kopeck (*hundredth of a rouble*)
корабль *m.* (**-ля**) ship, boat, vessel, craft (*ocean-going, esp. military*)
корзина/корзинка (*G pl.* **-нок**) basket (*large/small*)
коридор corridor, passage
коричневый brown (*not of eyes, hair or the body*)
кормить/на- *and* **по-** (**кормлю кормишь**) (+ *A* + *I*) to feed

25

Vocabulary

(*sb.* on *sth.* , *animals* with *sth.*), give (*sb. sth.*) to eat

коро́бка (*G pl.* **-бок**) box (*for sweets, shoes, etc.*)

коро́ва cow

короле́ва queen

коро́ль *m.* (**короля́**) king

коро́ткий (**ко́роток -тка́ -тки/ -тки́**; *comp.* **коро́че**) short (*in time or space*), brief; (*in short form with end stress*) too short (*of clothes*)

  ко́ротко briefly, in brief, in short

корреспонде́нт/-ка (*G pl.* **-ток**) correspondent, penfriend, penpal (*male/female*)

косми́ческий cosmic, space (*adj.*)

  косми́ческий кора́бль spacecraft, spaceship

космона́вт cosmonaut, astronaut, spaceman

ко́смос cosmos, (outer) space

(**косну́ться**: *see* **каса́ться**)

костёр (**костра́**) bonfire, campfire

кость *f.* (*pl.* **ко́сти -éй**) bone

костю́м suit, costume

кот (**кота́**) tom-cat

котёнок (**-ёнка**; *pl.* **котя́та -я́т**) kitten

котле́та chop, cutlet, rissole

кото́рый who, which, that, whose, to whom, *etc.* (*relat.*); which (*interrog.*)

  кото́рый час? what time is it?

ко́фе *m. indecl.* coffee

  ко́фе с молоко́м white coffee

кофе́йник coffee-pot

ко́фта (*woman's*) cardigan, (*loose-fitting*) jacket

ко́фточка (*G pl.* **-чек**) blouse, top

кошелёк (**-елька́**) purse (*Eng.*)

ко́шка (*G pl.* **ко́шек**) cat

край (**в/на краю́** *in 1st meaning*; *pl.* **края́ краёв**) edge; region, territory, land

кран tap, (*Amer.*) faucet, spigot; crane (*for building, etc.*)

краси́вый beautiful, handsome, good-looking, lovely

кра́сный red

  Кра́сная пло́щадь Red Square

красть/у- (**краду́ -ёшь**; **крал**) (+ *A* + **у** + *G*) to steal (*sth. from sb.*)

кра́ткий (**-ток -тка́ -тки**) short (*esp. of time*); brief, concise

  и кра́ткое (й) (*the name of the Russian letter* **й**)

Кремль *m.* (**-ля́**) the Kremlin

кре́пкий (**-пок -пка́ -пки**; *comp.* **кре́пче**) strong, sound, robust, firm

кре́сло (*G pl.* **-сел**) armchair

крестья́нин (*pl.* **-я́не -я́н**) peasant (*male*)

крестья́нка (*G pl.* **-нок**) peasant(woman), peasant girl

крик shout, cry

кри́кет cricket (*the sport*)

крича́ть (**-чу́ -чи́шь**)/**за-** *and* **кри́кнуть** (**-ну -нешь**) to cry (out), shout, yell, scream

крова́ть *f.* bedstead, bed (*as furniture*)

кровь *f.* blood

кро́ме (+ *G*) except; besides, as well as

кроссо́вки (**-вок**) running shoes, trainers, sneakers

кру́глый round

круго́м (+ *G*) round, around (*in a circle*); round about, all around (*adv.*)

кружо́к (**кружка́**) circle, society, group (*for study, etc.*)

кру́пный large, big, great (*important in scale*)

круто́й steep

крыло́ (*pl.* **кры́лья -ев**) wing

крыльцо́ porch; (entrance) steps

Крым (**в Крыму́**) the Crimea

кры́ша roof

кто (**кого́ кому́ кем ком**) who, whom, to whom, *etc.* (*interrog.*)

куда́ where (to)

ку́кла (*G pl.* **ку́кол**) doll

кукуру́за maize, (*Amer.*) corn, sweet corn

культу́ра culture

культу́рный (**-рен -рна**) cultured, cultivated

купа́льный костю́м bathing costume/suit, swimsuit, (swimming) togs

купа́ться/ис- *or* **вы́-** to bathe, have a bathe/swim, go swimming

купе́ *n. indecl.* compartment (*in train*)

(**купи́ть**: *see* **покупа́ть**)

кури́ть/по- (**-ю ку́ришь**) to smoke

    здесь не ку́рят no smoking (here)

pf. **закури́ть** to light (up) (*pipe, etc.*)

ку́рица (*pl.* **ку́ры кур**) hen; (*as food*) chicken

куро́рт (*use* **на**) (health/holiday) resort, spa

курс course (*of study*); year (*of study*)

    студе́нт пе́рвого ку́рса first-year student, freshman, fresher

ку́ртка (*G pl.* **-ток**) (*man's casual*) jacket, (*short*) coat, anorak, windcheater

кусо́к (**куска́**) piece, bit, lump, slice

куст (**куста́**) bush, shrub

ку́хня (*use* **в** *or* **на**) kitchen

ку́шать/по- to eat, have, take, try (*in polite usage, esp. in imp.*)

    ку́шайте, пожа́луйста do (please) help yourselves

лаборато́рия laboratory

ла́герь *m.* (*pl.* **-я -ей**) camp

ла́дно! all right, OK, righto

ла́мпа lamp, light (*usu. with shade*)

ла́сковый affectionate, tender, gentle, kind, soft

лати́нский Latin (*adj.*)

лгать/со- (**лгу лжёшь лгут; лгала́**) to lie, tell a lie/lies (*usu. more precise and stronger than* **врать**)

лев (**льва**) lion

ле́вый left, left-hand

лёгкий (**лёгок легка́**; *comp.* **ле́гче**) light (*not heavy*); slight; easy легко́ easily; it is easy

лёд (льда; на льду́) ice

(Ледови́тый: *see* Се́верный)

лежа́ть (-жу́ -жи́шь) to lie, be lying (down); to be (*in a lying position, e.g. of person in bed, books on a table*)

лежа́ть в больни́це to be (ill) in hospital

лезть/по- (ле́зу -ешь; лез ле́зла (в/на + *A*) to climb, crawl, get (into/onto *sth.*; *def.*)

лека́рство (от + *G*) medicine, drug, remedy (for *sth.*)

ле́кция (*use* на) lecture

чита́ть/слу́шать ле́кцию по геогра́фии to give, deliver/ attend, go to, listen to a geography lecture

лени́вый lazy, idle

Ленингра́д Leningrad

лес (в лесу́; *pl.* -а́ -о́в) forest, wood

ле́стница stairs, staircase; ladder

по ле́стнице up-/downstairs (*with motion*)

лета́ть to fly (*indef.*)

лете́ть/по- (лечу́ лети́шь) to fly, be flying (*def.*)

ле́тний summer (*adj.*)

ле́то summer

ле́том in (the) summer

pl. лета́ years (of age), age (*used as pl. of* год, *as below*)

ско́лько ему́ лет? how old/ what age is he?

ему́ два́дцать два го́да he is twenty-two (years old)/aged twenty-two

ему́ два́дцать пять лет he is twenty-five (years old)/aged twenty-five

лётчик airman, pilot (*as profession*; *cf.* пило́т)

ли whether, if (*in indirect questions*); interrog. particle

есть ли у тебя́ э́та кни́га? have you got/do you have this book?

лимо́н lemon

лимона́д lemonade; (lemon *or other*) squash

лине́йка (*G pl.* -еек) ruler

ли́ния line; policy

лиса́ *or* лиси́ца fox

лист (*pl.* -ы́ -о́в *and* ли́стья -ьев) (*first pl.*) sheet, page, leaf (*of paper, etc., two-sided*); (*second pl.*) leaf (*of tree, plant*)

литерату́ра (по + *D*) literature, publications, books (*on a subject*)

спи́сок литерату́ры reading list

литр litre

лифт lift, (*Amer.*) elevator

лицо́ (*pl.* ли́ца) face; person; character (*in play, etc.*)

ли́чный private, personal

ли́шний superfluous; unnecessary, not needed; too many/much; extra, spare, left over

нет ли у вас ли́шнего биле́та? have you a ticket you don't want/need?

лишь only; no sooner

лишь то́лько as soon as

лоб (лба; **на лбу**) forehead

ловить (ловлю ловишь)/
поймать to (try to) catch,
(*pf.*) to catch, take (*catch hold
of or capture*)
ловить рыбу to fish

лодка (*G pl.* лодок) boat (*esp. of
small varieties*)

ложиться/лечь (лягу -жешь
-гут; *imp.* ляг(те); лёг
легла) to lie (down); to go, get
in (*to bed, etc.*)
ложиться/лечь спать to go to
bed
лечь в больницу to go (in)to
hospital

ложка (*G pl.* ложек) spoon

ложь *f.* (лжи ложью) lie(s),
falsehood

локоть *m.* (локтя; *pl.* -и -ей)
elbow

ломать/с- to break (*sth. in two or
fracture*; *leg, arm, etc.*)
ломаться/с- to be broken,
break (*intrans.*); to break down
(*of car, machine*)

лошадь *f.* (*pl.* -ди -дей -дьми
and -дями) horse

луг (**на лугу**; *pl.* -а -ов) meadow

лук (*s. only*) onions

луна moon

луч (луча; *G pl.* лучей) ray, beam
(*of light*)

(лучше, лучший: *see* **хороший**)

лыжи (лыж) skis
ходить на лыжах to ski
лыжный спорт skiing

любимый favourite, beloved,
best(-loved)

любить/по- (люблю любишь) to
love, like, be fond of/keen on,
be/(*pf.*) fall in love with
больше любить to like better,
prefer
не любить to dislike, *etc.*
совсем не любить to hate,
strongly dislike

любовь *f.* (любви любовью) (к
+ *D*) love, strong affection
(of/for *sth./sb.*)

любой any (*of any kind*); anyone,
anybody (*no matter who*)

(люди: *see* **человек**)

Мавзолей (В. И.) Ленина the
Lenin Mausoleum

магазин shop, store
ходить/идти по магазинам to
go round the shops, go
shopping

магнитофон tape recorder
кассетный магнитофон
cassette recorder/player

май May

майка (*G pl.* маек) vest, singlet,
sports jersey, T-shirt, top

макароны (-он) macaroni

маленький (*for short forms use*
мал -а -ы; *comp.* меньше,
меньший) little, small; short
(*of stature*); young (*of
children*); (*only in short forms*)
too small, *etc.*

малина (*s. only*) raspberries

мало (+ *G*) little, not much, too
little (*sth.*); few, not many, too
few (*sth.*)

Vocabulary

ме́ньше (+ *G*) less, not so much
(*sth.*), fewer, not so many
(*sth.*)
  как мо́жно ме́ньше as little/
  few as possible
ма́льчик boy
ма́ма mum(my), ma
мандари́н mandarin, tangerine,
clementine
ма́рка (*G pl.* **ма́рок**) (postage-)
stamp; brand, make, model (*of
machine, car, etc.*)
март March
маршру́т itinerary, route
ма́сло butter; oil (*refined or
edible*)
ма́стер (*pl.* **-а́ -о́в**) master, expert
мастерска́я (**-о́й**) workshop,
(repair, *etc.*) shop; studio
матема́тика mathematics, maths,
(*Amer.*) math
матро́с sailor, seaman (*esp. a
naval rating*; *cf.* **моря́к**)
матч match, game (*the event*)
мать* *f.* mother
маши́на machine, engine; car,
(*Amer.*) automobile; lorry,
(*Amer.*) truck
машини́ст engine-driver, engineer
машини́стка (*G pl.* **-ток**) typist
маши́нка (*G pl.* **-нок**) (*as below*)
  (**пи́шущая**) **маши́нка**
  typewriter
  (**шве́йная**) **маши́нка** sewing-
  machine
ме́бель *f.* furniture
мёд honey
меда́ль *f.* medal
медве́дь *m.* bear

медици́нский medical
медици́нская спра́вка doctor's
  certificate/note, sick-note
ме́дленно slowly
медсестра́ (*pl.* **-сёстры**, *etc.*)
  nurse (*in hospital, etc.*)
ме́жду (+ *I.*) between, among
  ме́жду на́ми between
  ourselves/you and me
  ме́жду про́чим by the way, in
  passing, incidentally
  ме́жду тем meanwhile, (in the)
  meantime
  ме́жду тем, как while, whereas
междунаро́дный international
мел chalk
ме́лкий small (*coins, potatoes,
eggs, etc.*); fine (*sand, rain,
etc.*); shallow (*water*)
ме́нее (*adv.*) less (*with adj. or
adv.*)
  тем не ме́нее nevertheless,
  none the less, however
  (**ме́ньше, ме́ньший**: *see*
  ма́ленький, ма́ло)
меню́ *n. indecl.* menu
ме́ра measure
  по ме́ре возмо́жности as far as
  possible, as best one can
  по кра́йней ме́ре at least
мёртвый dead (*but cf.* **умере́ть**)
ме́стный local
ме́сто (*pl.* **места́**) place, spot, site,
locality; space (*for parking,
etc.*); seat (*in theatre, etc.*),
berth (*in ship, train*); job, post,
situation
  нет ме́ста there is no room
  на твоём ме́сте if I were you

ме́сяц month
в про́шлом/э́том/бу́дущем
ме́сяце last/this/next
month
мета́лл metal
мете́ль *f.* snowstorm, blizzard
метр metre
метро́ *n. indecl.* metro,
underground (railway), tube,
(*Amer.*) subway
меха́ник mechanic
мехово́й fur (*adj.*)
мечта́ (*for G pl. use* **мечта́ний**)
dream (daydream, desire)
мечта́ть (**о** + *P*) to dream (of/
about *sth., as desire, etc.*)
меша́ть/по- (+ *D* + *inf.*) to
prevent, hinder, stop (*sb. from*
doing sth.)
мешо́к (**мешка́**) sack, bag
милиционе́р policeman, police
officer (*in the USSR*)
мили́ция (*Soviet*) police
миллио́н million
ми́лый (**мила́**) nice, lovable,
sweet, dear
э́то о́чень ми́ло с твое́й
стороны́ that/it is very nice of
you
ми́ля mile
ми́мо (+ *G*) by, past (*of motion*
past; *adv. and prep.*)
минера́льные во́ды mineral
waters, minerals
ми́нус minus; drawback,
disadvantage
мину́та minute; moment
(**подожди́те**) **мину́ту/мину́тку/**
мину́точку! wait a minute/

moment, just a
minute/moment, hold on
мир 1 world; universe
весь мир all the/the whole
world
чемпио́н ми́ра world champion
мир 2 peace
ми́рный peace (*adj.*); peaceful
мирово́й world (*adj.*)
(**мла́дший**: *see* **молодо́й**)
мне́ние opinion
быть высо́кого/невысо́кого
мне́ния (**о** + *P*) to think
highly/not much (of *sb./sth.*)
мно́гие (**-их**) many (*adj. and*
pron.), many people
мно́гие из вас many of you
мно́го (+ *G*) much, many, a lot,
lots, plenty, a large amount, a
good/great deal (of *sth.*)
бо́льше (+ *G*) more (*sth.*), a
greater number/amount, (of
sth.)
бо́льше не(т) no more, not any
more, no longer
бо́льше всего́ most (of all),
more than anything
как мо́жно бо́льше as much/
many as possible
бо́льше того́ (and) what is
more
мно́гое (**-ого**) many things, a lot
(of things)
мо́да fashion, vogue
мо́дный fashion (*adj.*);
fashionable, stylish
мо́жет быть maybe, perhaps
не мо́жет быть! it can't be! it's
not possible! impossible!

31

мо́жно one may, one can, one is allowed to

мо́жно войти́? may I/we come in?

как мо́жно скоре́е as quickly/ soon as possible

мой* my; mine

мо́крый wet, moist

мо́лния lightning

молодёжь *f.* young people, youth (*collectively*)

молоде́ц (-дца́) a fine fellow/girl

молоде́ц! well done! bravo!

молодо́й (мо́лод -а́ -ы; *comp.* моло́же; мла́дший) young; youthful; new (*of vegetables, wine, etc.*); (*only in short forms*) too young, *etc.*

мла́дший younger, youngest; junior

мо́лодость *f.* youth (*period of life*)

молоко́ milk

мо́лча in silence, silently, without a word

молча́ть (-чу́ -чи́шь) to be/keep quiet/silent, say nothing

pf. **замолча́ть**, *etc.* to fall silent, stop talking

моме́нт moment, instant

моне́та coin; change (*coins*)

мопе́д moped

мо́ре (*pl.* моря́ -е́й) sea

мо́рем by sea

на мо́ре (*A*) to the seaside

на мо́ре (*P*)/**у мо́ря** at the seaside, by the sea

морко́вь (*no pl.*) *f. or* **морко́вка** carrot(s)

моро́женое (-ого) ice(-cream)

моро́з frost; freezing weather

морско́й marine, naval, sea (*adj.*)

моря́к (-яка́) sailor, seaman (*the general term; cf.* **матро́с**)

Москва́ Moscow

моско́вский Moscow (*adj.*)

мост (на мосту́; *pl.* -ы́ -о́в) bridge

моте́ль *m.* motel, motor inn/ lodge

мотоци́кл motor cycle, motor bike

мочь/с- (могу́ мо́жешь мо́гут; мог могла́) can, to be able; may, to be allowed to

я не могу́ не (+ *inf.*) I can't help (*doing sth.*)

му́дрый (мудра́) wise

муж husband

мужско́й man's, men's, boy's, boys', male, masculine

мужчи́на *m.* man (*as opposed to woman*), male

музе́й museum

му́зыка music

музыка́льный musical, music (*adj.*)

музыка́нт/-ша musician, player (*male/female*)

му́ха fly

мы (нас нам на́ми нас) we; us, *etc.*

мы́ло soap

мысль *f.* thought, idea

мыть/вы- *or* **по- (мо́ю -ешь; вы́мою, *etc.*)** to wash (*trans.*)

мы́ться/вы- to wash (oneself), have a wash, get washed

мышь *f.* (*pl.* -и -е́й) mouse

Vocabulary

мя́гкий (мя́гок мягка́ -и; *comp.*
мя́гче) soft; gentle, mild

мя́со meat

мяч (мяча́) ball (*that bounces*)

на 1 (+ *A*) onto, on; into, to (*a place*; *used instead of* **в** *with certain nouns*); 2 (+ *P*) on; in, at (*a place*; *used instead of* **в** *with certain nouns*); 3 (+ *A*) for (*a period to come*); on, at (*a day or festival time*); 4 (+ *P*) by (*transport, e.g. car, bus*)

наве́рно *or* **наве́рное** (very) probably, most likely

наве́рх upstairs, up (*to a higher floor; adv.*)

наверху́ upstairs, up (*on a higher floor; adv.*)

навсегда́ for ever, for good

навстре́чу (*adv. and prep.* + *D*) to meet (*used as below*)

ве́тер дул навстре́чу the wind was against us/them, *etc.* /was blowing from the opposite direction

навстре́чу нам шёл ма́льчик a boy was coming towards us/ to meet us

награ́да reward, award, prize

над (+ *I*) over, above (*of position or motion*)

надева́ть/наде́ть (-е́ну -е́нешь) to put on (*clothes, spectacles*)

наде́жда hope, expectation

наде́яться (-е́юсь -е́ешься) (на + *A*) to hope (for *sth.*); to rely (on *sb.*)

на́до *or* **ну́жно** it is necessary, one

must/has (got) to/ought/ should, one needs

ему́ на́до (ну́жно) рабо́тать he must/needs to work, *etc.*

мне на́до (ну́жно) молока́/ ты́сячу рубле́й I need milk/a thousand roubles

не на́до! you shouldn't/mustn't; don't!

надое́л /-а/-о/-и (*from* **надое́сть**) one is bored, fed up (with), tired/sick (of) (*used as below*)

мне надое́ла ужа́сная пого́да I'm fed up with the awful weather

мне надое́ло слу́шать поп- му́зыку I'm tired of listening to pop music

наза́д back, backwards

(тому́) наза́д ago, previously

назва́ние name (*of place or thing*), title (*of book, etc.*)

называ́ться to be called/named/ entitled (*of place, thing, book, etc.*)

как называ́ется э́та у́лица? what is the name of this street?

наизу́сть (*adv.*) by heart, from memory

нака́зывать/наказа́ть (накажу́ -а́жешь) (+ *A* + **за** + *A*) to punish (*sb.* for *sth.*)

накану́не (+ *G*) the day before, on the eve (of *sth.*; *adv. and prep.*)

наконе́ц at last, finally, in the end

накрыва́ть/накры́ть (накро́ю -о́ешь) (на) стол to lay/set the table

33

Vocabulary

нале́во (от + G) (to the) left (*with motion*; *adv.*); to the left, on the left (of *sth.*; *prep.*)

налива́ть/нали́ть (налью́ -ьёшь; на́лил -а́ -и; *imp.* **нале́й(те))** to pour (out); to fill

наоборо́т on the contrary

напада́ть/напа́сть (нападу́ -ёшь; напа́л) (на + A) to attack (*sb./sth.*)

напи́ток (-тка) (*kind of*) drink, beverage

напомина́ть/напо́мнить (+ D + о + P or + D + A) to remind (*sb. of sth.*)

  она́ напо́мнила мне о собра́нии she reminded me of the meeting

  она́ напо́мнила мне мою́ мать she reminded me of my mother (*i.e. was like her*)

направле́ние direction (*of movement*)

  по направле́нию (к + D) in the direction (of), towards

напра́во (от + G) (to the) right (*with motion*; *adv.*); to the right, on the right (of *sth.*; *prep.*)

напра́сно in vain, to no purpose, for nothing; wrongly, unjustly, mistakenly

наприме́р for example, for instance, e.g.

напро́тив (+ G) opposite (*adv. and prep.*), over the way, across the road/street

наро́д people, nation; people (*as a group*)

мно́го наро́ду a lot of people

наро́дный national, people's, popular, folk (*adj.*)

наро́чно on purpose, purposely, intentionally, deliberately

насеко́мое (-ого) *nn.* insect

на́сморк (head) cold (*illness*)

насто́льный те́ннис table-tennis, ping-pong

настоя́щий real, true, genuine; present (*of time*)

  в настоя́щее вре́мя at present, at the present time, at the moment, nowadays

  настоя́щее (-его) the present (*nn.*)

настрое́ние mood, temper, humour, frame of mind

нау́ка science; study, learning

нау́чный scientific, science, research (*adj.*)

  нау́чная фанта́стика science fiction

находи́ть (нахожу́ -о́дишь)/ найти́ (найду́ -ёшь; нашёл нашла́) to find, discover

находи́ться to be (situated)

национа́льность *f.* nationality (*separate ethnic group within the USSR, etc.*)

национа́льный national (*relating to the preceding*)

нача́ло beginning, start, outset

в нача́ле (+ G) in/at the beginning (of), early in (*year, month, etc.*)

нача́льник head, chief, superior, commander, boss, manager

начина́ть/нача́ть (начну́ -ёшь;

34

на́чал -а́ -и) (+ *A* / *impf. inf.*) to begin, start (*sth./doing sth.*)

начина́ться, *etc.* (*but* **начался́ -а́сь -и́сь**) to begin, start (*intrans.*)

наш* our; ours

не not

не́ за что! don't mention it, not at all, that's all right

не́бо (*pl.* **небеса́ небе́с -а́м**) sky, heaven

небольшо́й small, little, not very big, not great, not large; short (*esp. of time*)

Нева́ the Neva (*river*)

нева́жно not too well, indifferently

(я) чу́вствую себя́ нева́жно I don't feel too good/so well

невозмо́жно it is impossible/can't be done

невысо́кий not high, low; short, not tall; poor, low (*of quality, opinion, etc.*)

неда́вно recently, not long ago

недалеко́ (от + *G*) not far (away from), quite near/close (to), a short way/distance (from/to *sth.*; *adv. and prep.*)

неде́ля week

на про́шлой/э́той/бу́дущей неде́ле last/this/next week

не́жный (не́жен -жна́ -ы) tender, soft, affectionate

нездоро́вый unwell, not well, poorly, not feeling well (*in short forms*)

не́когда there is no time/isn't time

мне не́когда (гуля́ть, *etc.*) I've

no time/haven't time (to go for a walk, *etc.*)

не́который some, certain

некраси́вый ugly, plain, not very good-looking, not beautiful, unattractive

некульту́рный (-рен -рна) uncivilized, uneducated, ignorant; bad-mannered, rough, boorish, rude

нельзя́ it is impossible, one cannot; one must/may not, one is not allowed, it is forbidden

здесь кури́ть нельзя́ no smoking (here)

нема́ло (+ *G*) a good deal, a considerable amount, quite a lot, a good/fair number (of)

неме́дленно immediately, straightaway, forthwith

неме́цкий German (*adj.*)

не́мец (не́мца) German (*male*)

не́мка (*G pl.* **не́мок**) German (*female*)

немно́го (+ *G*) *or* **немно́жко** (*coll.*) not much, little, (only) a little; not many, few, (only) a few; for a short time, for a little while; a little, somewhat, slightly, rather

ненави́деть (-ви́жу -ви́дишь) to hate, loathe, detest

необходи́мый necessary, essential

неожи́данный unexpected, sudden

непра́вда untruth, lie, falsehood

непра́вда, что ... it is not true that . . .

э́то непра́вда that isn't true, that's wrong

непра́вильно wrong(ly), incorrectly

не́сколько (+ *G*) several, some, (quite) a few

несмотря́ на (+ *A*) despite, in spite of

несомне́нно without doubt, undoubtedly, doubtless, without fail

(нести́: *see* **носи́ть)**

несча́стный unhappy, unfortunate, unlucky

несча́стье misfortune; accident

к несча́стью unfortunately, unluckily

нет 1 no; yes (*when negating a negative*; *cf.* **да**)

(нет 2: *see* **быть**)

неуже́ли? really, can it be true, is it possible, surely not?

нефть *f.* (petroleum) oil

не́чего (не́ о чем, *etc.*) there is nothing to

ей не́чего чита́ть she has nothing to read

ни … ни … **(не)** neither … nor …

ни (оди́н) (не) not one, not a single, not any

(-нибудь: *see* **-то)**

нигде́ (не) nowhere, not anywhere (*in no place*)

ни́зкий (*comp.* **ни́же,** *comp. and superl.* **ни́зший**) low

ни́зко low, low down (*adv.*)

ника́к (не) in no way, by no means, not at all

никако́й (не) no, not any

никогда́ (не) never, not ever

никто́ (никого́, *etc.*) **(не)** no one, not anyone, nobody, not anybody

никуда́ (не) nowhere, not anywhere (*to no place*)

ничто́ (ничего́, *etc.*) **(не)** nothing, not anything

ничего́ that's all right, it doesn't matter, never mind; not bad(ly), all right, so-so, can't complain

но but

Но́вая Зела́ндия New Zealand

новозела́ндец (-дца) New Zealander (*male*)

новозела́ндка (*G pl.* **-док**) New Zealander (*female*)

новозела́ндский New Zealand (*adj.*)

но́вости (-е́й) news

s. **но́вость** *f.* (piece of) news

но́вый new; fresh, recent

нога́ (но́гу, ноги́; *pl.* **но́ги ног -а́м)** leg; foot

нож (ножа́) knife

ноль (ноля́) *and* **нуль (нуля́)** *m.* nought (naught), zero, 0, nil

но́мер (*pl.* **-а́ -о́в**) number (*of house, bus, telephone, shoes, etc.*); issue, number (*of magazine, etc.*); room (*in hotel*)

норма́льный (-лен -льна) normal, standard (*adj.*)

норма́льно normally; as it should; (it is) OK, all right

нос (в/на носу́) nose

носи́льщик porter

носи́ть (ношу́ но́сишь) (*indef.*) to carry, take, bring (*by carrying*); to wear (*as a rule*; *cf. usage under* **в**)

нести́/понести́ (несу́ -ёшь; нёс несла́) (*def.*) to carry, take, bring (*by carrying*)

носо́к (носка́) sock
  па́ра носко́в a pair of socks

ночева́ть (ночу́ю -ешь) to spend/pass the night, overnight

ночно́й nocturnal, night (*adj.*)

ночь *f.* (*pl.* **но́чи ноче́й**) night
  час/2, 3 часа́ но́чи 1, 2, 3 a.m.
  но́чью at night, in the night
  (вчера́) но́чью last night, during the night

ноя́брь *m.* (**-бря́**) November

нра́виться/по- (+ *D*) to please
  мне нра́вится, *etc.* I like, *etc.*
  кни́га мне не понра́вилась I didn't like/disliked the book

ну well, well now, well then

(ну́жно: *see* **на́до)**

ну́жный (-жен -жна́ -жно -жны́) necessary, required, needed, wanted
  нам ну́жен холоди́льник we need a refrigerator
  она́ нужна́ здесь she is wanted here, we need her here, *etc.*

(нуль: *see* **ноль)**

о (об, обо *before some letters*) 1 (+ *P*) about, concerning, of, on (the subject of); 2 (+ *A*) on, upon, onto, against (*of falling, hitting, etc.*)

о́ба *m. and n.* /**о́бе** *f.* (**обо́их**, *etc.* / **обе́их**, *etc.*; *behaves like* **два**) both (*adj. and pron.*)

обе́д dinner *or* (*full*) lunch, midday meal; dinner-time, lunch-time (*i.e. around midday*)
  по́сле обе́да after dinner/ lunch; in the afternoon, this afternoon
  за́втра по́сле обе́да tomorrow afternoon

обе́дать/по- to dine, have (one's) dinner *or* to lunch, have/take (one's) lunch

обезья́на monkey, ape

обеща́ть *impf. and pf.* (+ *D* + *A*) to promise (*sb. sth.*)

о́блако (*pl.* **-á -óв -áм**) cloud

о́бласть *f.* (*pl.* **-и -éй**) oblast, province, region; field, sphere, realm, domain

обме́нивать/обменя́ть (на + *A*) to change, exchange (*e.g. one currency* into/for *another*)

о́браз way, manner
  каки́м о́бразом? (in) what way, how?
  таки́м о́бразом (in) this/that way, so, thus
  гла́вным о́бразом mainly, chiefly, principally, for the most part, mostly

образова́ние education

обра́тный return (*adj.*; *of ticket, etc.*); reverse, opposite (*direction, etc.*)
  на обра́тном пути́ on the way back

обра́тно back (*adv.*; *of returning or replacing*)

туда́ и обра́тно there and back; return, round trip (*of ticket*)

обраща́ть/обрати́ть (-щу́ -ти́шь) внима́ние (на + *A*) to pay/give attention (to), note, notice, take note/notice (of), look at (*attentively*)

обсужда́ть/обсуди́ть (-жу́ -у́дишь) to discuss, review, consider, talk over

о́бувь (*s. only*) *f.* footwear; shoes, boots (*collectively*)

общежи́тие hostel, hall of residence, (*Amer.*) dormitory

обще́ственный social, public

о́бщество society, company, association

о́бщий common, general

в о́бщем in general, on the whole, all in all

объясня́ть/-ни́ть to explain

обыкнове́нный *or* **обы́чный** usual, ordinary, customary, everyday

обы́чно *or* **обыкнове́нно** usually, as a rule, generally

как обы́чно as usual

обяза́тельно without fail, certainly, I've got to, they have to, one absolutely must, *etc.*

о́вощи (-е́й) vegetables

овца́ (*pl.* о́вцы ове́ц о́вцам) sheep; ewe

ого́нь *m.* (огня́) fire (*in stove, etc.*); light (*which can be lit*)

огоро́д (vegetable-)garden, kitchen-garden

огро́мный (-мен -мна) very great, huge, vast, enormous

огуре́ц (огурца́) cucumber, gherkin

одева́ться/оде́ться (оде́нусь -ешься) to dress (oneself), get dressed

оде́жда clothes, clothing

оде́тый (в + *A*) clothed, dressed (in *sth.*)

одея́ло blanket, quilt

оди́н/одна́/одно́/одни́* one; a, an, a certain; by oneself, alone; only, nothing but; (one and) the same

оди́н из нас one of us

одни́ ... други́е ... some ... others

оди́ннадцатый eleventh

оди́ннадцать eleven

одна́жды once, one day

одна́жды у́тром, *etc.* one morning, *etc.*

одна́ко however, but, (and) yet, though

ожида́ть to wait (for), await, expect, anticipate

о́зеро (*pl.* озёра) lake

ока́зываться/оказа́ться (окажу́сь ока́жешься) to find oneself (*esp. in an unexpected place*); to turn out/prove (to be)

она́ оказа́лась хоро́шей актри́сой she proved a good actress

оказа́лось, что мы учи́лись

38

вме́сте в шко́ле it turned out that we had been to school together

ока́нчивать/око́нчить to conclude, complete, end, terminate, finish, graduate from (*university, school*)

океа́н ocean

окно́ (*pl.* **о́кна о́кон**) window

о́коло (+ *G*) near, close to, by (*beside*); about, around

оконча́ние conclusion, completion, end, termination

   по оконча́нии шко́лы/ университе́та on/after leaving/graduating from school/university

октя́брь *m.* (**-бря́**) October

октя́брьский October (*adj.*)

   Вели́кая Октя́брьская социалисти́ческая револю́ция the Revolution (*of October 1917*)

олимпи́йский Olympic

омле́т omelette

он/она́/оно́/они́* he/she/it/they; him, her, them, *etc.*

опа́здывать/опозда́ть (на + *A*) to be late (for *sth.*), to miss (*sth. by being late*)

опа́сный dangerous, perilous

о́пера opera; opera-house

опера́ция operation

опи́сывать/описа́ть (опишу́ -и́шешь) to describe

опуска́ть/опусти́ть (опущу́ -у́стишь) to lower, let down; to drop

опусти́ть письмо́ в я́щик to post a letter (in the box)

опусти́ть моне́ту в автома́т to drop/insert a coin in the (call) box/machine/slot

о́пыт experiment, test; experience

опя́ть again

организа́ция organization

   Организа́ция Объединённых На́ций (ООН) United Nations Organization (UNO)

организова́ть *impf. and pf.* (**-зу́ю -ешь**) to organize; to plan (*one's time, work*)

оре́х nut (*edible*)

орке́стр orchestra; band

ору́жие (*s. only*) weapons, arms

осе́нний autumn (*adj.*)

о́сень *f.* autumn, (*Amer.*) fall

   о́сенью in (the) autumn/the fall

осма́тривать/осмотре́ть (осмотрю́ -о́тришь) to examine, survey, inspect; to look round, see, do (*museum, sights, etc.*)

осо́бенный especial, special, particular

остава́ться (остаю́сь -ёшься)/ оста́ться (оста́нусь -ешься) to remain, stay, be left (over)

оставля́ть/оста́вить (-влю -вишь) to leave, leave behind, abandon, quit

оста́вь(те)! stop it/that, lay off

остально́й the rest/remainder of, remaining

   остальны́е the others, the rest

остана́вливать/останови́ть

39

(-овлю́ -о́вишь) to stop, halt (*trans.*), bring to a stop/halt

остана́вливаться, *etc.* to stop, halt (*intrans.*), come to a stop/halt; to stop working (*of machines*); to stop, stay, put up (*at a hotel, etc.*)

остано́вка (*G pl.* **-вок**) stop (*bus-stop, etc.*)

осторо́жный (**-жен -жна**) careful, cautious

осторо́жно! careful! take care! look out!

о́стров (*pl.* **-á -óв**) island

о́стрый (**остёр остра́ о́стры**) sharp, pointed; keen

от (**ото** *before certain groups of consonants*; **+ G**) from, away from; for, of, with, to (*various senses of cause or relationship*)

отве́т answer, reply, response, solution

отвеча́ть/отве́тить (**-чу -тишь**) (**+ D/на + A**) to answer, reply, respond ((to) *sb./a question, letter, etc.*)

отдава́ть/отда́ть (**от + дава́ть/да́ть** *but* **о́тдал(и) -á**) to give back, return (*sth.*)

отде́л section, department, counter (*of shop, business, etc.*)

отделе́ние department, branch (*of company, institution*); (police) station

отде́льный separate, detached, individual

о́тдых rest; recreation; holiday

отдыха́ть/отдохну́ть (**-ну́ -нёшь**) to rest, have/take a rest, (be on) holiday, have/take a holiday

оте́ц (**отца́**) father

оте́чественный home, of one's own country; patriotic

Вели́кая Оте́чественная война́ World War Two (*from the Soviet standpoint, 1941–5*)

отка́зываться/отказа́ться (**откажу́сь -а́жешься**) (**от + G/+ inf.**) to refuse, decline (*sth./to do sth.*)

открыва́ть/откры́ть (**откро́ю -бешь**) to open (*trans.*); to turn on (*tap*)

открыва́ться, *etc.* to open (*intrans.*), be opened

откры́тка (*G pl.* **-ток**) (post)card

откры́тый open

отку́да where from, from which

отлича́ться (**от + G**) to differ from, be different from

отли́чный (**-чен -чна**) excellent, extremely good

отли́чно! excellent! (also = **пятёрка**)

отме́тка (*G pl.* **-ток**) mark, grade (*result*)

отноше́ние relation(ship)

отправля́ть/отпра́вить (**-влю -вишь**) to send

отправля́ться, *etc.* to leave, set off/out, start (out), go (*on a journey, etc.*)

о́тпуск holiday(s), (*Amer.*) vacation, leave (of absence from work; *cf.* **кани́кулы**)

ле́тний о́тпуск summer holiday(s)/vacation

в о́тпуске on holiday/vacation

отря́д detachment, working-party (*of Pioneers, etc.*)

отсу́тствовать (-ствую -ешь) (на + *P*) to be absent/away/ missing (from *a lesson, etc.*)

отсю́да from here, from this (place), hence

отту́да from there, from that (place)

отходи́ть (отхо́дит)/отойти́ (отойдёт; отошёл) to leave, depart (*of train, bus*)

о́тчество patronymic (*Russian middle name, formed from father's first*)

отъе́зд departure

офице́р officer

официа́нт/-ка (*G pl.* -ток) waiter/waitress

охо́та hunting, shooting

охо́тно gladly, willingly, readily

очарова́тельный (-лен -льна) charming, fascinating, captivating

очеви́дно obviously, evidently

о́чень very, very much, greatly, highly, ever so

о́чередь *f.* turn (*next in order*); queue, line

по о́череди in turn, in order

стоя́ть в о́череди (за + *I*) to queue (up)/stand in line (for *sth.*)

очки́ (очко́в) spectacles, glasses, goggles

ошиба́ться/-би́ться (ошибу́сь

-ёшься; оши́бся -блась) to make a mistake/mistakes, err, be mistaken/wrong/in the wrong/at fault

оши́бка (*G pl.* -бок) mistake, error, fault, slip, blunder

па́дать/упа́сть (упаду́ -ёшь; упа́л) to fall, fall down, drop

паке́т parcel, packet, (paper) bag

пала́тка (*G pl.* -ток) tent

па́лец (па́льца) finger; toe

большо́й па́лец thumb; big toe

пальто́ *n. indecl.* (over)coat, topcoat

па́мятник monument, memorial, statue (*in memory of sb.*)

па́мятник Чайко́вскому a monument to/statue of Tchaikovsky

па́мять *f.* memory

на па́мять from memory; as a keepsake/souvenir

па́па *m.* dad(dy), pa

папиро́са cigarette (*Russian-style with cardboard holder*)

па́ра pair; couple

па́рень *m.* (па́рня) (young) lad, boy; fellow, chap, bloke, guy

парикма́хер (*coll. f.* -ша) barber, hairdresser

парикма́херская (-ой) barber's (shop), hairdresser's, hairdressing salon

парк park

парк культу́ры и о́тдыха recreation park/ground

парохо́д steamer, (steam)ship, (steam)boat, liner

па́рта (school) desk

па́ртия party (*esp.* the Party)

Коммунисти́ческая па́ртия Сове́тского Сою́за (КПСС) the Communist Party of the Soviet Union (CPSU)

па́русный спорт sailing

па́спорт (*pl.* -а́ -о́в) passport; (*for Soviet citizens*) national identity card

пассажи́р passenger

па́сха Easter, Passover

на па́сху at/for Easter(tide)

па́хнуть (**па́хнет -нут; пах па́хла**) (+ *I*) to smell (of *sth.*)

па́чка (*G pl.* **па́чек**) bundle, parcel, packet, pack (*of cigarettes, papers, books, etc.*)

певе́ц (**певца́**)/**певи́ца** singer (*male/female*)

пе́ние singing; (bird)song

пе́нсия pension

пе́нсия по ста́рости old-age pension

на пе́нсии on a pension, retired

уйти́ на пе́нсию to retire (*from work*)

пе́рвый first

пе́рвого января́ on the first of January

Пе́рвое ма́я May Day, the First of May

пе́рвое (-ого) *nn.* first course (*of meal*)

что на пе́рвое? what's the first course? what's for starters?

перево́д translation, interpretation; transfer, remittance

почто́вый перево́д postal order (*money transfer sent by post office*)

переводи́ть/перевести́ (**пере + води́ть/вести́**) (**с** + *G* + **на** + *A*) to translate, render, interpret (from *one language* to *another*)

перево́дчик/-чица translator, interpreter (*male/female*)

пе́ред (**передо** *with* **мно́й**; + *I*) in front of, before (*of position or motion*); (just) before (*time*)

передава́ть/переда́ть (**пере + дава́ть/да́ть** *but* **пе́редал(и) -а́**) to pass, pass on, hand, hand over, give (*into sb. else's hands*); to convey, communicate, pass on, tell (*message, news, etc.*)

переда́ть по ра́дио/ телеви́дению to broadcast/ televise

переда́ча broadcast, programme (*on radio or television*)

пере́дняя (-ней) (entrance) hall, lobby, anteroom

переезжа́ть/перее́хать (**-е́ду -е́дешь**) to cross, go/come/ ride/drive/travel across/over (*not on foot*); to move (house), remove, shift (*from one place to another; intrans.*)

переме́на change, alteration; break, recess, interval (*in school day*)

перепи́сываться to correspond, be in correspondence

переры́в interval, break (*from*

42

work, *between lectures, for
lunch, etc.*)

переса́дка (*G pl.* **-док**) change (*of
train, etc.*)

  без переса́дки without
changing, straight through

**переса́живаться/пересе́сть
(переся́ду -дешь; пересе́л)**
to change (*trains, etc.*)

**переставать (-стаю́ -ёшь)/
переста́ть (-а́ну -ешь)** (+
impf. inf.) to stop, cease, leave
off, quit (*doing sth.*)

перестро́йка reconstruction,
restructuring, reorganization,
reform

перехо́д crossing, passage (*over or
under street, etc.*)

  подзе́мный перехо́д
(pedestrian) subway/
underpass

**переходи́ть (-ожу́ -о́дишь)/
перейти́ (перейду́ -дёшь;
перешёл -шла́)** to cross, go/
come/walk across/over (*under
own power*)

перо́ (*pl.* **пе́рья -ьев**) feather,
plume; pen (*now chiefly
abstract*)

перча́тка (*G pl.* **-ток**) glove

пе́сня (*G pl.* **пе́сен**) song, air,
carol, *etc.*

песо́к (песка́) sand

петь/с- *and* **за- (пою́ поёшь)** to
sing (*2nd pf.* to begin to sing)

печа́льный (-лен -льна) sad,
mournful, melancholy

пече́нье (*use s. only*) (*sweet*)
biscuit(s), (*Amer.*) cookie(s)

пе́чка (kitchen-)range, oven,
stove

печь *f.* (**в/на печи́**) stove, boiler

пешехо́д pedestrian, foot-
passenger

пешко́м on foot

пиани́но *n. indecl.* (upright) piano

пи́во beer, ale

пиджа́к (-ака́) (*man's short suit-
type*) coat, jacket

пижа́ма (*use s. only*) pyjamas

пило́т pilot (*of a particular
aircraft*; *cf.* **лётчик**)

пионе́р/-ка (*G pl.* **-рок**) Pioneer
(*male/female*)

пионе́рский Pioneer (*adj.*)

пиро́г (-а́) pie, tart

пиро́жное (-ого) (*small or fancy*)
cake, pastry

пирожо́к (-жка́) (*small*) pie,
pastry, patty

писа́тель *m.* writer, author

писа́ть/на- (пишу́ пи́шешь) to
write; to paint (*pictures*)

  писа́ться to be spelt

  как пи́шется? how is it spelt/
do you spell it?

письмо́ (*pl.* **пи́сьма пи́сем**) letter
(*missive*)

пить/вы́пить (пью пьёшь; *imp.*
пей(те); пил(и) пила́/вы́пью,
etc.) to drink; to have, take
(*drink*)

пи́ща (*no pl.*) food

пла́вание swimming

  (пла́вательный) бассе́йн
(swimming) pool

пла́вать (*indef.*) to swim; to float;
to sail

плыть (плыву́ -ёшь; плыла́) (*def.*) to swim; to float; to sail

пла́кать/за- (пла́чу -ешь) to cry, weep

пла́мя *n.** flame(s)

план plan, scheme, schedule, programme; map, plan (*of town, etc.*)

пласти́нка (*G pl.* -нок) (gramophone) record, disc

плати́ть/за- (плачу́ пла́тишь) (+ *D*/за + *A*) to pay (*sb./for sth.*)

плато́к (платка́) headscarf, kerchief, shawl; handkerchief

платфо́рма platform

пла́тье (*G pl.* пла́тьев) (*woman's*) dress, frock, gown

плащ (плаща́) raincoat, mackintosh, waterproof

племя́нник nephew

племя́нница niece

плёнка (*G pl.* -нок) film (*photographic, etc.*); tape (*for recording*)

плечо́ (*pl.* пле́чи плеч -а́м) shoulder

плита́ *or* пли́тка cooker, stove

плохо́й (пло́х(-и)-а́; *comp.* ху́же, ху́дший) bad, wretched, nasty; poor (*health, results, etc.*)

пло́хо/ху́же bad(ly)/worse (*adv.*)

мне пло́хо I feel bad/ill, don't feel good/well

тем ху́же so much the worse, too bad, hard luck, tough!

переме́на к ху́дшему a change for the worse

площа́дка (*G pl.* -док) (play)ground, pitch, court (*for games, etc.*)

спорти́вная площа́дка sports ground, playing area

пло́щадь *f.* (*pl.* -ди -де́й) square, place (*in a town*)

(плыть: *see* пла́вать)

плюс plus; advantage

пляж beach

по (+ *D*) (*motion*) along, on (*river, road*), on, over (*floor, grass, ice*), (a)round, about, through (*room, streets, town, etc.*); on, over (*telephone, radio, television*); by (*post, rail, etc.*); according to, by (*with respect to, etc.*); in, on (*mornings, Mondays, etc.*)

това́рищ по ко́мнате roommate

по- (*prefix used, as well as forming standard pfs, to impart the sense* a little, *as e.g. below*)

посиде́ть/постоя́ть to sit/stand a little/for a time/while

полежа́ть to have a lie-down/rest

порабо́тать to do a bit of work

поспа́ть to have a nap/little sleep, sleep a bit

по-англи́йски/-ру́сски/-францу́зски, *etc.* in English/Russian/French, *etc.*

говори́ть/чита́ть/писа́ть/понима́ть по-ру́сски, *etc.* to speak/read/write/understand Russian, *etc.*

по-ва́шему (-тво́ему)/-мо́ему/

-нашему in your/my/our opinion, to your/my/our mind/way of thinking; as you/ I/we want/wish/would like

побе́да victory, conquest, win, triumph

повора́чивать/поверну́ть (-ну́ -нёшь) to turn (*trans.*); to turn (*change one's course*; *intrans.*)

повора́чиваться, *etc.* to turn (*intrans.*)

повторя́ть/-ри́ть to repeat, reiterate, say/do again; to review, revise, go over, rehearse (*lesson, homework, role, etc.*)

пого́да weather

кака́я сего́дня пого́да? what is the weather (like) today?

сего́дня хоро́шая пого́да it is fine today

под (подо *with* **мно́й, всём,** *etc.*; + *A/I*) under, underneath, beneath, below; near, in the vicinity/environs of (*a town*; *motion/position*)

под дождём in the rain

пое́хать на да́чу под Москву́ to go to a dacha outside Moscow

жить под Москво́й to live in the Moscow area

под ве́чер towards evening

подава́ть/пода́ть (по + дава́ть/ дать *but* **по́дал(и) -а́)** to serve (up) (*drink, meal, etc.*); to hand in, lodge, send (in)

пода́рок (пода́рка) gift, present

подборо́док (-дка) chin

подзе́мный underground, subterranean

поднима́ть/подня́ть (подниму́ -ни́мешь; по́дня́л(и) -а́) to pick up, lift, raise

поднима́ться, *etc.* (*but* **подня́лся́ -ла́сь -ли́сь**) (**на** + *A*) to rise, get/go/come up, ascend, climb (*sth., e.g. hill*)

поднима́ться на ли́фте to go up in the lift/elevator, take the lift/elevator (up)

подно́с tray

подо́бный similar, such, like (*of the same kind*)

ничего́ подо́бного nothing of the kind

подпи́сывать/подписа́ть (подпишу́ -пи́шешь) to sign (*document, etc.*)

подпи́сываться, *etc.* to sign (one's name)

по́дпись *f.* signature

подража́ть (+ *D*) to imitate, copy (*sb./sth.*)

подро́бность *f.* detail

подру́га friend (*female*)

поду́шка (*G pl.* **-шек**) pillow, cushion

подходи́ть (подхожу́ -о́дишь)/ подойти́ (подойду́ -дёшь; подошёл -шла́) (к + *D*) to approach, walk/go/come up to (*sb./sth.*; *under own power*); (+ *D*) to suit, be suitable (for), fit, go with, do for (*sb./ sth.*)

подъéзд entrance, doorway, porch (*where vehicles stop*)

пóезд (*pl.* **-á -óв**; *use* **в** *or* **на**) train

    éхать пóездом to go by train

поéздка (*G pl.* **-док**) trip, outing, tour, journey

пожáлуй very likely, probably, it may well be, I think so

    пожáлуй, онú уéхали I think they must have gone

пожáлуйста please; please do, certainly (you may), by all means; that's all right; you're welcome, not at all, don't mention it

пожáр fire (*destructive*)

пожáрный *or* (*coll.*) **пожáрник** fireman, firefighter

поживáть (*used as below*)

    как (вы) поживáете? how are you?

пожилóй elderly, getting on in years

позавчерá (on) the day before yesterday

позадú (*adv. and prep.* + *G*) behind

позволя́ть/позвóлить (+ *D* + *inf.*) to allow, let, permit (*sb.* (*to*) *do sth.*)

    позвóльте предстáвить (вам) мою́ сестру́ allow me to introduce my sister (to you)/ you to my sister

пóздно late (*adv.*); it is late; it is too late

    comp. **пóзже** later, later on, at a later date

поздравлéния (**-ий**) congratulations

поздравля́ть/поздрáвить (**-влю -вишь**) (+ *A* + **с** + *I*) to congratulate (*sb.* on *sth.*); to wish (*sb. sth.*)

    поздравля́ю (вас) с Нóвым гóдом! I wish you a happy New Year

(**поймáть**: *see* **ловúть**)

покá for now/the present/the time being; while, for as long as

    покá не not (as) yet; until, till, before

    покá! see you later/soon, so long, cheers, cheerio, 'bye

покáзывать/показáть (**покажу́ -áжешь**) to show, display

покрывáть/покры́ть (**покрóю -óешь**) to cover

    покры́тый (+ *I*) covered (with *sth.*)

покупáтель *m.* customer, client, buyer, purchaser

покупáть/купúть (**куплю́ ку́пишь**) to buy, purchase, get (*by buying*)

покýпки (**-пок**) shopping, errands, purchases

    ходúть/идтú за покýпками *or* **дéлать покýпки** to shop, go/ do the shopping

пол (**на полу́**) floor (*as surface*)

пóлдень *m.* (**полу́дня**) midday, noon, twelve (o'clock)

пóле (*pl.* **-я́ -éй**) field

    спортúвное пóле sports ground, playing field

поле́зный (-зен -зна) useful, helpful; healthy, good (for one)

полёт flight

поликли́ника polyclinic, clinic

поли́тика politics; policy

полити́ческий political

полице́йский (-ого) policeman, police officer (*in non-Communist countries*)

поли́ция police (*in non-Communist countries*)

по́лка (*G pl.* по́лок) shelf

по́лночь *f.* (полу́ночи) midnight, twelve (o'clock at night)

по́лный (по́лон -лна́ -лны) full; complete, total, entire; stout, plump, corpulent, portly

по́лно! that will do! enough (of that)!

полови́на half

три с полови́ной three and a half

сейча́с полови́на пе́рвого *or* полпе́рвого, *etc.* it is (now) half-past twelve, *etc.*

в полови́не пе́рвого, *etc.* at half-past twelve, *etc.*

положе́ние position, location, whereabouts, situation

(положи́ть: *see* класть)

полоте́нце (*G pl.* -нец) towel

полтора́ *m. and n.* / полторы́ *f.* (полу́тора) one and a half; a . . . and a half

полтора́ часа́ one hour and a half, ninety minutes

полтора́ го́да eighteen months

полторы́ неде́ли a week and a half, ten days (or so)

получа́ть/получи́ть (-чу́ -у́чишь) to receive, obtain, get, have

полчаса́ (получа́са) half an hour, a half hour

помидо́р tomato

по́мнить (*for pf. use* вспо́мнить) (+ *A or* о + *P*) to remember, bear/keep in mind, recollect, recall

помога́ть/помо́чь (по + мо́чь) (+ *D*) to help, assist, aid (*sb.*)

по́мощь *f.* help, assistance, aid, relief

ско́рая по́мощь first aid; ambulance (service)

понеде́льник Monday

понима́ть/поня́ть (пойму́ -ёшь; по́нял(и) -ла́) to understand, realise, see, comprehend; to know about, be a (good) judge of

непра́вильно понима́ть to misunderstand, mistake, get wrong

пойми́ меня́ don't misunderstand me, don't get me wrong

поня́тно clearly, intelligibly; it is clear/natural/understandable; is that clear? (do you) see?; I see, understood, of course

попада́ть/попа́сть (-аду́ -ёшь; -а́л) to get to/into, reach, arrive at

как попа́сть в Кремль? how does one get to/what is the way to the Kremlin?

поп-му́зыка pop music, pop

популя́рный (**-рен -рна**) popular,
  well-liked
пора́ time (*period, season*)
  с каки́х пор? since when?
  с тех/э́тих пор since then/that
    time
  с тех пор, как (ever) since
    (*conj.*)
  до каки́х пор? till when? until
    what time? how long?
  до тех пор, пока́ (не) for as
    long as (*in neg.* until, till; *conj.*)
  до сих пор up to now, until
    now, hitherto
  пора́ (+ *inf.*) it is time (*to do
    sth.*)
  (давно́) пора́ домо́й it's (high)
    time to go/be getting home
порт (**в порту́**) port, harbour
портре́т portrait, likeness, picture
  (*of sb.*); portrayal, depiction,
  character sketch
портфе́ль *m.* (brief)case, (school)
  bag (*with handle*)
(по-ру́сски: *see* **по-**)
поря́док (**-дка**) order
  (*arrangement or sequence*)
  всё в поря́дке everything is all
    right, all correct, OK
посеща́ть/посети́ть (**-щу́ -ти́шь**)
  to visit, call on, frequent; to go
  to, see (*museum, etc.*); to
  attend (*lectures*)
поскоре́е! (be) quick! hurry (up)!
(посла́ть: *see* **посыла́ть**)
по́сле (+ *G*) after, since (*prep.*);
  after(wards), later (on) (*adv.*)
  по́сле того́, как after (*conj.*)
после́дний last, final; latest

послеза́втра (on) the day after
  tomorrow
посреди́ (+ *G*) in the middle/
  midst (of), among
посте́ль *f.* (*use* **в**, *but* **с** + *G*)
  bed (*bedding in which one
  sleeps*)
  лечь в посте́ль to get into bed,
    go to bed (*to read, etc.*)
  встать с посте́ли to get out of
    bed, get up (from bed)
постепе́нно little by little, bit by
  bit, gradually, by degrees
постоя́нный constant, continual,
  permanent, perpetual
поступа́ть/-пи́ть (**-плю́ -у́пишь**)
  (**в/на** + *A*) to enter, go to,
  start (at) (*school, university,
  etc.*), join (*army, etc.*)
посу́да crockery, plates and
  dishes; (kitchen) utensils; (tea,
  etc.) things
  мыть посу́ду to wash up, do the
    washing-up, wash/do the
    dishes
посудомо́ечная маши́на *or*
  (*coll.*) **посудомо́йка**
  dishwasher (*washing-up
  machine*)
посыла́ть/посла́ть (**пошлю́
  -шлёшь**) to send, dispatch
  посла́ть по по́чте to post, mail
посы́лка (*G pl.* **-лок**) parcel (*sent
  by post*)
потоло́к (**-олка́**) ceiling
пото́м then, after that; afterwards,
  later (on)
потому́ что because, as
(по-францу́зски: *see* **по-**)

похо́ж/-а/-е/-и (на + *A*) (*used as below*)

он похо́ж на отца́ he is like/ looks like/resembles/bears a resemblance to his father

вы о́чень похо́жи друг на дру́га you are very much alike/very like each other

э́то на неё не похо́же that's not like her

похо́же (на то, что) it appears/ would appear/looks like (*sth. will happen, etc.*)

почему́ why, what . . . for

по́чта post office; post, mail

на по́чте at the post office

по по́чте by post/mail

почтальо́н postman, postwoman, postie, mailman, *etc.*

почти́ almost, nearly, practically, virtually

почти́ ничего́ hardly/scarcely anything

почто́вый postal, postage, post, mail (*adj.*)

почто́вый я́щик letter-box, mail-box, pillar-box, post(ing)-box

почто́вая бума́га note-paper, writing-paper, letter-paper

поэ́т poet

поэ́тому therefore, and so, that's why

появля́ться/появи́ться (-влю́сь -я́вишься) to appear, emerge, come in(to) sight/view, come out; to make/put in an appearance, show (up)

пра́вда (the) truth; (it is) true

пра́вда? really? indeed? is that so?

не пра́вда ли? isn't it? aren't you? didn't he? *etc.*

пра́вило rule, regulation, principle

как пра́вило as a rule, normally

пра́вильный right, correct, true, proper; regular

пра́вильно! that's right! just so! exactly! precisely!

прави́тельство government

пра́во (*pl.* -а́) law (*esp. as a subject*); right (*to do sth., etc.*)

име́ть пра́во (на + *A*) to have the right/be entitled (to *sth.*)

води́тельские права́ driving licence

пра́вый right, right-hand

прав/права́/пра́вы right, correct

ты прав/не прав you are right/wrong

пра́здник (public/bank) holiday; (*religious*) festival, feast(-day); (festive) occasion

с пра́здником! congratulations!; season's greetings! compliments of the season!

пра́чечная (-ой) laundry (*the place*)

пра́чечная самообслу́живания laund(e)rette, laundromat, washeteria

предлага́ть/предложи́ть (-жу́ -о́жишь) to propose, suggest, offer

Vocabulary

предложе́ние proposal, suggestion, offer

предме́т object, article, item; subject (*of study*), theme, topic

председа́тель *m.* chairman, president

представля́ть/предста́вить (-влю -вишь) to introduce, present

представля́ть себе́ to imagine, fancy, picture, conceive

пре́жде before, formerly, once, first

пре́жде всего́ first of all, before anything else, to begin with

пре́жде чем before (*conj.*)

прекра́сный (-сен -сна) beautiful, fine, fair; excellent, splendid, first-rate, capital

прекра́сно! very good, excellent, splendid

преподава́тель *m.* teacher, instructor, (junior/assistant) lecturer (*in higher/tertiary education*)

преподава́ть (-даю́ -ёшь) to teach, lecture in/on (*subj. in higher education*)

при (+ P) in the presence of, in (my, *etc.*) presence, in front of, before; attached to, at, in (*of one place or institution joined with another*); on, by, about, with (*of sth. carried with one*); under, in the time/days/reign of (*ruler, government, famous person, etc.*)

приближа́ться/прибли́зиться (-жусь -зишься) (к + D) to approach, near, come/get/draw near(er) ((to) *sth./sb.*)

приве́т greeting(s), regards; hallo! hi!

приводи́ть/привести́ (при + води́ть/вести́) to bring (*sb. on foot*)

привози́ть/привезти́ (при + вози́ть/везти́) to bring, fetch, bring back (*sb. or sth. – presents, etc.*; *not on foot*)

привыка́ть/привы́кнуть (-ну -нешь; привы́к -ла) (к + D / + inf.) to get used, become accustomed, get into the habit/way of (*pf.* to be used/accustomed, *etc.*) (to *sth./sb./(to) doing sth.*)

привы́чка (*G pl.* -чек) habit, custom, practice

приглаша́ть/пригласи́ть (-шу́ -си́шь) to invite, ask

приглаше́ние invitation

приду́мывать/приду́мать to invent, make/think up, devise

прие́зд arrival

приезжа́ть/прие́хать (прие́ду -дешь) (в/на + A) to arrive (at), come (to *a place*; *not on foot*)

прие́м (*use* на) reception, party

часы́ прие́ма hours of attendance; surgery hours, consultation times

прика́з order, command

прика́зывать/приказа́ть (прикажу́ -а́жешь) (+ D + inf.) to order, command, direct, tell (*sb. to do sth.*)

Vocabulary

приключе́ние adventure
прилета́ть/-те́ть (-лечу́ -ти́шь)
to fly in, arrive (*of aircraft or passengers*)
приме́р example, instance, model
принадлежа́ть (-жу́ -жи́шь) (+ D; + к + D) to belong (*to sb.*); to belong to, be a member of (*club, etc.*)
принима́ть/приня́ть (приму́ при́мешь; при́нял(и) приняла́) to receive, accept, admit, see (*receive*); to take, have (*food, medicine, bath, shower*); to take, make, adopt (*decision, measure, etc.*)
приноси́ть/принести́ (при + носи́ть/нести́) to bring, fetch, deliver (*sth. on foot*)
приро́да nature
прису́тствовать (-ствую -ешь) (на + P) to attend, be present (at)
присыла́ть/присла́ть (пришлю́ -шлёшь) to send, dispatch
притворя́ться/-и́ться (+ I) to pretend (to be *ill, etc.*), feign (*sth.*)
приходи́ть (-ожу́ -о́дишь)/ прийти́ (приду́ -дёшь; пришёл -шла) (в/на + A, к + D) to arrive (at), come, get (to *a place*/to see *a person*; *under own power*)
прихо́дится (приходи́лось)/ придётся (пришло́сь) (+ D) have to, need to, must (*used like* на́до)

причёска (*G pl.* -сок) haircut, hair-do, hair style, the way one does one's hair
причёсываться/причеса́ться (причешу́сь -че́шешься) to comb/brush/do one's hair; to have/get one's hair done, have a hair-do
причи́на (+ G) cause, reason, motive (of/for *sth.*)
причи́на в том, что ... the reason is that ...
прия́тель *m.*/-ница friend, close acquaintance, pal, mate, buddy/(female) friend, girl-friend, lady-friend
прия́тный (-тен -тна) nice, pleasant, pleasing, agreeable
мне прия́тно слу́шать её I like/enjoy listening to her
прия́тно вас ви́деть I'm happy/glad to see you
о́чень прия́тно! how do you do? (I'm very) pleased to meet you
про (+ A) about, of (*speak, etc.*, concerning *sb./sth.*)
про себя́ to oneself (*of reading, talking, etc.*)
пробле́ма problem
про́бовать/по- (про́бую -ешь) to try, attempt, endeavour (*to do sth.*); to try, try out, test, taste, feel (*i.e. try*)
проверя́ть/прове́рить to check, verify, examine, test
проводи́ть/провести́ (про + води́ть/вести́) to spend, pass (*time*)

51

как ты провела́ вре́мя? what sort of time did you have? did you have a good time?

провожа́ть/проводи́ть (-ожу́ -о́дишь) (на + A, до + G, etc.) to see (off), take, accompany, walk (*sb. home, see off on journey*)

прогно́з пого́ды weather forecast

програ́мма programme, syllabus, curriculum, schedule; (*TV*) channel

прогу́лка (G pl. -лок) walk, stroll, ramble; trip, outing, ride, drive, sail, row, *etc.*

продава́ть/прода́ть (про + дава́ть/да́ть but про́дал(и) -а́) to sell

продаве́ц (-вца́)/-вщи́ца seller, shop-assistant, store clerk, salesman/-woman

прода́жа sale

в прода́же on/for sale

продово́льственный магази́н *or* **продма́г** foodshop, food store, grocery (store), foodmart

продолжа́ть/продо́лжить to continue, proceed, go on, keep (on) ((*with*) *sth., doing sth.*)

продолжа́ться, *etc.* to continue (*intrans.*), go on, be in progress, last (*for a stated period*)

проду́кты (-ов) produce, provisions, groceries, food(stuffs)

проезжа́ть/прое́хать (-е́ду -е́дешь) (ми́мо + G, etc.) to pass, go/come/ride/drive/travel (past/by/through; *not on foot*); to drive, cover (*a certain distance*); to go past, miss (*bus-stop, etc.*)

скажи́те, пожа́луйста, как прое́хать на Кра́сную пло́щадь? can you please tell me how to get to Red Square?

прои́грыватель *m.* record-player, compact disc/CD player, gramophone

прои́грывать/проигра́ть to lose (*of games, war, etc.*)

производи́ть/-вести́ (произ- + води́ть/вести́) to produce, turn out, create, make

произноси́ть/произнести́ (произ- + носи́ть/нести́) to pronounce, utter, say (*articulate*); to make, give, deliver (*speech*)

как произно́сится э́то сло́во? how is this word pronounced? how do you pronounce this word?

произноше́ние pronunciation

происходи́ть (происхо́дит)/ произойти́ (произойдёт; произошло́) to happen, occur, take place, be going on

промы́шленность *f.* industry

пропада́ть/пропа́сть (-аду́ -ёшь; -а́л) to disappear, vanish; (*pf.*) to be lost/missing, to be wasted, to have gone (*in vain*)

где ты пропа́л? where have you been? where (on earth) were you?

про́пуск (*pl.* **-а́ -о́в**) pass, permit
(*to go somewhere*)

проси́ть/по (**прошу́ -о́сишь**)
(**+ A + inf.; y + G + A/G**)
to ask, beg, request (*sb. to
do sth.*); to ask (*sb. for
sth.*)

проспе́кт view, avenue, drive (*type
of city street*)

(**прости́ть**: *see* **проща́ть**)

просто́й (**про́ст(ы) -а́**; *comp.*
про́ще) simple, easy; plain,
common, ordinary; unaffected;
mere

про́сто simply, merely, purely,
just

про́сто так for no particular
reason, just like that

просту́да (chest) cold, chill

простужа́ться/-ди́ться (**-жу́сь
-у́дишься**) to get/catch (a)
cold, take a chill, (*pf.*) have a
cold

простыня́ (*pl.* **про́стыни -сты́нь
-я́м**) (bed)sheet

просыпа́ться/просну́ться (**-ну́сь
-нёшься**) to wake (up), awake
(*intrans.*)

про́сьба request; favour (*to ask*)

про́тив (**+ G**) against; opposite,
facing

я ничего́ не име́ю про́тив
(**э́того**) I have nothing against
(it), I don't mind

профе́ссия occupation, trade,
profession

**кто вы по профе́ссии/кака́я у
вас профе́ссия?** what is your
profession/line of work?

я по профе́ссии учи́тель I am
a teacher by profession, I
teach

профе́ссор (*pl.* **-а́ -о́в**) professor

профсою́з (trade) union

прохла́дный (**-ден -дна**) cool,
fresh (*of weather*)

проходи́ть (**-ожу́ -о́дишь**)/
пройти́ (**пройду́ -дёшь;
прошёл -шла́**) (**ми́мо + G,
etc.**) to pass, go/come/walk
(past/by/through; *under own
power*); to pass, go (by),
elapse, (*pf.*) be over (*of time*);
to go (away), (*pf.*) be gone (*of
pain, illness, etc.*); to let up,
abate, cease, stop (*of rain,
etc.*); to go (off) (*well, etc.; of
events*)

**скажи́те, пожа́луйста, как
пройти́ на вокза́л?** can you
please tell me how to get to the
station?

проце́нт percentage; (bank)rate,
interest

сто проце́нтов a hundred per
cent

(**про́чий**: *see* **ме́жду**)

про́шлый past; last (*preceding*)

про́шлое (**-ого**) the past (*nn.*)

проща́й(те) goodbye, farewell

проща́ть/прости́ть (**прощу́
-сти́шь**) to forgive, pardon,
excuse

прости́(те) (меня́)! sorry!
pardon! excuse me! I beg your
pardon!

проща́ться/по- *or* **прости́ться**
(**-щу́сь -сти́шься**) (**с + I**) to

say goodbye (to *sb.*) to take
leave (of *sb.*)

пры́гать/пры́гнуть (**-ну -нешь**)
to jump, leap, bounce

прямо́й (**пря́м(ы) пряма́**)
straight, direct,
straightforward, frank, blunt

пря́мо (*adv.*) straight, direct (*of
travelling*); upright, erect (*of
standing, etc.*); frankly, *etc.*

пря́таться/с- (**пря́чусь -чешься**)
to hide (oneself), conceal
oneself

пти́ца bird

пуга́ть/ис- *and* **на-** to frighten,
scare, startle, intimidate

пуга́ться, *etc.* to be frightened,
etc., take fright

пуло́вер pullover (*usu. V-neck*)

пуска́ть/пусти́ть (**пущу́
пу́стишь**) to let, allow, permit
(*sb. to do sth.*); to let (*sb./sth.*)
go, let go (of *sth./sb.*)

пусто́й (**пуст(ы) пуста́**) empty;
hollow; vain, pointless

пусты́ня desert, wilderness

пусть let (*used in forming 3rd pers.
imp.*)

**пусть она́ (с)де́лает, что
хо́чет** let her do what she
wants

путёвка (*G. pl.* **-вок**) (travel)
pass, voucher (*for holiday or
sick leave*), (tickets for a) trip
abroad

путеше́ствие voyage, journey,
cruise, (long) trip, tour

путь *m.* (*G/D/P* **пути́** *I* **путём**; *pl.*
-и́ -е́й) way, path, track

отпра́виться в путь to set out
(on a journey/trip)

по пути́ (домо́й) on the way
(home)

счастли́вого пути́! bon voyage,
have a good trip

каки́м путём? in what way? by
what means?

пшени́ца wheat

пылесо́с vacuum (cleaner)

пыль *f.* (**в пыли́**) dust

пыта́ться/по- (+ *inf.*) to attempt,
try, endeavour (*to do sth.*)

пье́са play (*dramatic*)

пья́ный (**пьяна́**) drunk, drunken,
intoxicated, tipsy, tight; (*as
nn.*) a drunk

пятёрка (*G pl.* **-рок**) a five, top
mark, excellent, A (*in Soviet 5-
point marking system*)

пятидеся́тый fiftieth

пятна́дцатый fifteenth

пятна́дцать fifteen

пя́тница Friday

пятно́ (*pl.* **пя́тна пя́тен**) spot,
stain, blot, patch, blemish

пя́тый fifth

пять (**пяти́**) five

пятьдеся́т (**пяти́десяти**) fifty

пятьсо́т (**пятисо́т -ста́м**) five
hundred

рабо́та work, labour, employment,
job

на рабо́те at work (*on the
premises*)

за рабо́той at work (*on the job*)

рабо́тать (**над** + *I*) to work (on, at
sth.); to work, function,

operate, run (*of machines, etc.*); to be open (*of library, museum, etc.*)

не рабо́тать not to work, be out of order; to be closed (*of library, museum, etc.*)

рабо́тник/-ница worker, employee (*male/female*; *white-collar or agricultural*)

нау́чный рабо́тник (research) worker/scientist

рабо́чий working, workers', work (*adj.*); (*as nn.*) worker, workman, working man, hand, labourer (*industrial, etc.*)

ра́вный (-вен -вна́ -вны́) equal

всё равно́ (it is) all the same, it makes no difference

нам всё равно́ it's all the same to us, we don't mind/care

рад/ра́да/ра́ды (+ D) glad, pleased (of/by/with *sth.*)

она́ ра́да мои́м успе́хам she is pleased with my progress

о́чень рад! (I'm very) pleased to meet you

ра́ди (+ G) for the sake of, for (*sb.'s*) sake

ра́ди бо́га! for god's/heaven's/goodness' sake!

ра́дио *n. indecl.* radio, radio set, wireless

по ра́дио on the radio, over the air, by radio

ра́доваться/об- (-дуюсь -ешься) (+ D) to rejoice, be happy (at/in *sth.*)

ра́достный (-тен -тна) joyful, glad, happy; good (*news, etc.*)

ра́дость *f.* joy, gladness

раз (*G pl.* **раз**) time, occasion

в пе́рвый раз for the first time

в после́дний раз for the last time

в сле́дующий раз next time

в друго́й раз another/some other time

на э́тот раз this time (*adv.*), on this occasion, for (this) once

раз, два, три ... one, two, three ...

(оди́н) раз one time, once

два ра́за twice

раз в неде́лю once a week

ещё раз (once) again

не раз more than once

ни ра́зу (не) not once, never

ка́ждый/вся́кий раз, когда́ whenever, every time that

как раз exactly, precisely, just

разбива́ть/разби́ть (разобью́ -бьёшь; *imp.* **разбе́й(те))** to break (in pieces), smash, crash, shatter (*trans.*)

разбива́ться, *etc.* to break, *etc.* (*intrans.*), (*pf.*) be broken, *etc.*

ра́зве really? is it/can it be true (that)? (*but often not transl. in Eng.*; *expresses surprise or criticism*)

разгова́ривать to speak, talk, converse, have a talk

разгово́р talk, conversation

раздава́ться (-даётся)/разда́ться (-да́стся -даду́тся; -да́лся -ла́сь) to sound, be heard, ring (out)

раздева́ться/-де́ться (-де́нусь -де́нешься) to undress, get undressed, strip (oneself); to take off one's things (*coat, hat, gloves, etc.*)

(разли́чный: *see* **ра́зный)**

разме́р size; measurements, dimensions

  како́го разме́ра? what size?

  како́й ваш разме́р? what size do you take?

  костю́м со́рок шесто́го разме́ра a size 46 suit

ра́зница difference

ра́зный *or* **разли́чный** different, differing, diverse, various (kinds of)

разочаро́ванный (-ван -вана) (в + *P*) disappointed, disillusioned (by/with/in *sth.*)

разреша́ть/-ши́ть (+ *D* + *inf.*) to allow, permit, let (*sb. do sth.*)

  разреши́те пройти́! excuse me, may I come past, please?

  разреши́те предста́вить (вам) мою́ сестру́ allow me to introduce my sister (to you)/ you to my sister

разреше́ние permission, authorization

разуме́ется it/that goes without saying, obviously, of course

райо́н raion; district, area, vicinity

раке́та rocket, missile; hydrofoil

ра́неный wounded, injured; (*as nn.*) wounded/injured person, casualty

ра́нний early

ра́но early (*adv.*); it is early; it is too early (*to do sth.*)

  ещё ра́но it's still too early, it isn't time yet

ра́ньше earlier (on), sooner; before; formerly, in the past

  как мо́жно ра́ньше as early/ soon as possible

расписа́ние timetable, schedule

  расписа́ние уро́ков (school) timetable

  расписа́ние движе́ния поездо́в, *etc.* train/railway timetable, *etc.*

расска́з story, short story, tale; account, narrative

расска́зывать/-сказа́ть (-ажу́ -а́жешь) to tell, relate, account, narrate

расте́ние plant (*that grows*)

расти́/вы́- (расту́ -ёшь; рос росла́/вы́расту, *etc.*) to grow, increase; to grow up; to rise (*of prices, etc.*)

расчёска (*G pl.* -сок) comb

рвать/разо- *and* **со- (рву рвёшь; рвала́)** (*1st pf.*) to tear; (*2nd pf.*) to pick, pluck (*flowers*)

ребёнок (-ёнка; *pl.* **ребя́та -я́т** *and* **де́ти дете́й де́тям детьми́ де́тях)** child; infant, baby (*2nd pl. standard here; 1st used mainly for addressing children*); (*1st pl.*) lads, boys, guys

револю́ция revolution

ре́гби *n. indecl.* rugby (football), rugger

56

ре́дко (*comp.* **ре́же**) rarely, not (very) often, seldom, infrequently

ре́зать/по- *or* **от-** (**ре́жу ре́жешь**) (*1st pf.*) to cut (*make a cut, e.g. on one's finger*); (*2nd pf.*) to cut (off), slice (*e.g. a piece of bread*)

результа́т result, outcome

река́ (**ре́ку реки́**; *pl.* **ре́ки рек река́м**) river

рели́гия religion

ремо́нт repair(s), maintenance (**закры́т**) **на ремо́нт** closed for repairs, under repair

респу́блика republic

рестора́н restaurant

реце́пт recipe; (doctor's) prescription

речь *f.* (*pl.* **ре́чи рече́й**) speech **о чём речь?** what is the question/subject? what are you talking about/ discussing?

    речь идёт о то́м, . . . the point/ question is . . .; we are discussing . . .

реша́ть/реши́ть to decide, resolve, determine, make up one's mind (*to do sth.*); to solve, settle (*problem, etc.*)

реше́ние decision, solution

рис rice

рисова́ние drawing, art (*the subject*)

рисова́ть/на- (**рису́ю -ешь**) to draw, sketch; to paint (*esp. in water-colours*)

рису́нок (**-нка**) drawing (*picture*)

ро́бкий (**-бок -бка́ -бки**) timid, shy

ро́вный (**-вен -вна́ -вны**) flat, level, even, regular, smooth **ро́вно в два часа́** at two o'clock exactly/precisely/sharp/on the dot

    ро́вно ничего́ absolutely nothing

род kind, sort **како́го ро́да?** what kind of? **вся́кого ро́да** (+ *G*) of all kinds, all kind(s) (of *sth.*) **что́-то в э́том ро́де** something of the kind/to that effect

ро́дина (*use* **на**) one's (mother) country, native land, home(land)

роди́тели (**-ей**) parents

роди́ться *pf.* (**-ла́сь**) to be born

родно́й native, home, mother (*adj.*); own, blood-related; (*pl. as nn.*) relatives, relations, one's (own) people, kin

ро́дственник relative, relation, kinsman

(**рожде́ние**: *see* **день**)

рождество́ Christmas **на рождество́** at Christmas (-time), for Christmas **с рождество́м!** merry/happy Christmas!

рожь *f.* (**ржи ро́жью**) rye

ро́зовый pink

ро́лики (**-ов**) roller-skates

роль *f.* (*pl.* **-и -е́й**) role, part

рома́н novel

роня́ть/урони́ть (**-ю́ -о́нишь**) to drop, let fall

Росси́я Russia
рост height, stature
  како́го ро́ста? how tall? what height?
  высо́кого ро́ста tall, big (*in height*)
  ни́зкого ро́ста short, small
ро́стбиф roast beef
рот (рта; во рту́) mouth
роя́ль *m.* (grand) piano
руба́шка (*G pl.* -шек) shirt
  ночна́я руба́шка nightdress, nightgown, nightie
рубль *m.* (**рубля́**) rouble
ружьё (hand-)gun, rifle, shotgun
рука́ (**ру́ку руки́**; *pl.* **ру́ки рук -а́м**) arm; hand
ру́сский (*f.* **ру́сская**) Russian (*adj. and nn.*)
ру́сский язы́к Russian (language; *see also* **по-**)
ру́чка (*G pl.* **ру́чек**) pen (biro, *etc.*); handle, knob
ры́ба fish
ры́жий red/ginger-haired; red, ginger (*of hair*)
ры́нок (**ры́нка**; *use* **на**) market (-place)
рю́мка (*G. pl.* **рю́мок**) (wine)glass
ряд (**в ряду́**; *pl.* **-ы́ -о́в**) row, line; series, a number (of)
ря́дом (quite) close/near (by), next door, side by side
  ря́дом с (+ *I*) next to, beside, by (the side of), by (*sb.'s*) side

с (**со** *before certain groups of consonants*) 1 (+ *G*) from, off, down from (*also used instead of* **из** *where* **на** *is used instead of* **в**); 2 (+ *G*) since, (as) from, beginning from/in; 3 (+ *I*) with; 4 (+ *A*) about (*size, distance*)
  она́ начнёт рабо́тать здесь с понеде́льника she will start working here on Monday
  хлеб с ма́слом bread and butter
  мы с тобо́й you and I
  что с тобо́й? what's up/the matter with you?
  прие́хать с после́дним авто́бусом to come on/by the last bus
  я прошёл с киломе́тр I walked about a kilometre
сад (**в саду́**; *pl.* **-ы́ -о́в**) garden
  фрукто́вый сад orchard
сади́ться (**-жу́сь -ди́шься**)/**сесть** (**ся́ду -ешь; сел**) (**в/на** + *A, etc.*) to sit (down), be seated, take a seat; to board, take, get on (to)/in(to) (*train, bus, etc.*)
(сала́зки: *see* **са́нки)**
сала́т lettuce; salad
  сала́т из помидо́ров/огурцо́в tomato/cucumber salad
сам* myself, yourself, himself *etc.* (*emphatic pron.*)
самова́р samovar (*Russian water-heater for making tea*)
самолёт aeroplane, (air)plane, aircraft, airliner
  лете́ть на самолёте/ самолётом to fly, go by air

самообслу́живание self-service
магази́н самообслу́живания
self-service store
са́мый (*see also* **тот**) most, -est
(*superl.*); the very
са́мый лу́чший the very best
са́мый люби́мый one's very
favourite
до са́мого конца́ to the very
end, right to the end
са́ни (сане́й) sledge, sleigh
са́нки (са́нок) *or* **сала́зки (-зок)**
toboggan, sledge (*children's*)
сантиме́тр centimetre; tape-
measure
сапоги́ (сапо́г -а́м) (high) boots;
top-boots, wellingtons,
gumboots
са́хар sugar
све́жий (свежа́ -жи́) fresh; cool
(*wind*); new, latest, recent
(*news, etc.*); clean (*underwear*)
сего́дня свежо́ it is fresh/cool/
chilly today
свет 1 light (*natural or artificial*)
со́лнечный свет sunlight,
sunshine
свет 2 world, earth
путеше́ствие вокру́г све́та a
journey round the world
Но́вый свет the New World
свети́ть (све́тит) to shine (*of sun,
moon, stars*)
све́тло- light, pale (*added to adjs.
of colour*)
све́тлый bright, light, light-
coloured, fair
светло́ it is (day)light
светофо́р traffic light(s)

свида́ние (*use* **на**) meeting,
appointment, date, rendezvous
до свида́ния! goodbye
до ско́рого (свида́ния)! see
you soon, be seeing you
свинья́ (*pl.* **сви́ньи -не́й**) pig; sow
сви́тер (*coll. pl.* **-а́ -о́в**) (*high-
necked*) sweater, pullover,
jersey, sweatshirt
свобо́да freedom, liberty
свобо́дный (-ден -дна) free;
spare, off (*of time*); spare,
vacant, unoccupied (*seat, etc.*)
свобо́дно говори́ть по-ру́сски
to speak Russian fluently, be
fluent in Russian
свой* one's (own); his, her, its;
their; my; our; your (*must
refer back to subj. of relevant
verb*)
связь *f.* (**в связи́**) connection,
relation, link, tie;
communication
сдава́ть/сдать (с + дава́ть/дать)
to sit (for), take (*examination,
exam subj.*; *in pf. means also*
to pass)
сда́ча change (*money rendered*)
10 копе́ек сда́чи 10 kopecks
change
сеа́нс performance, house,
showing (*of film, etc.*)
себя́ (себе́ собо́й себе́) oneself;
myself, yourself, himself, *etc.*
(*refl. pron. for all pers.*)
се́вер (*use* **на**) north
Се́верная Ирла́ндия Northern
Ireland
Се́верное мо́ре the North Sea

се́верный north (*adj.*), northern, northerly

Се́верный Ледови́тый океа́н the Arctic (Ocean)

сего́дня today

сего́дня у́тром this morning

сего́дня ве́чером this evening, tonight

седо́й grey-/white-haired; grey, white (*of hair*)

седьмо́й seventh

сейча́с now, right now, at the moment, at present; just, just now (*in past*); presently, (very) soon; (*often reinforced with* же) at once, immediately, straightaway

сейча́с! just a moment! in a minute! coming!

секре́т secret

секрета́рь *m.* (-аря́)/-а́рша secretary (*male or female/ female*)

секу́нда second (*of time*); moment

село́ (*pl.* сёла) village (*larger than* дере́вня)

се́льский country, village (*adj.*), rural

семе́стр semester, half(-year), term (*two per year*)

семидеся́тый seventieth

семна́дцатый seventeenth

семна́дцать seventeen

семь (семи́) seven

се́мьдесят (семи́десяти) seventy

семьсо́т (семисо́т -ста́м) seven hundred

семья́ (*pl.* се́мьи семе́й) family

сентя́брь *m.* (-бря́) September

серди́тый (на + *A*) angry, cross (with *sb.*, at/about *sth.*)

серди́ться/рас- (сержу́сь се́рдишься) (на + *A*) to be/get/become angry/cross (with *sb.*, at/about *sth.*), lose one's temper

се́рдце heart

середи́на middle

се́рый grey; dull, drab

серьёзный (-зен -зна) serious, grave, earnest

сестра́ (*pl.* сёстры сестёр сёстрам) sister; nurse (*see* медсестра́)

(сесть: *see* сади́ться)

Сиби́рь *f.* Siberia

сигаре́та cigarette (*Western-style*)

сиде́ть (сижу́ сиди́шь) to sit, be sitting (down/seated); to be (*in a sitting position*); to stay, be (*for a certain time, e.g. at home*); to be (in prison)

сиди́(те)! don't get up, stay sitting down, remain seated

си́ла strength, force, power, might

изо всех сил with all one's strength, as fast/hard/loud, *etc.*, as one can (*depending on verb used*)

си́льный (силён сильна́ си́льны́) strong, powerful; heavy (*rain, etc.*); bad (*cold in the head*); intense, fierce (*heat*); hard, severe (*frost, etc.*); good (*in a subject*)

симпати́чный (чен -чна) likeable, nice, attractive

она́ мне о́чень симпати́чна I like her very much

си́ний (sea/dark) blue

си́ять to shine (brightly)

(**сказа́ть**: *see* **говори́ть**)

ска́зка (*G pl.* **-зок**) (*popular*) tale, story; fairy-story

наро́дные ска́зки folk-tales

скаме́йка (*G pl.* **-éек**) bench, seat (*in park, etc.*)

ска́терть *f.* (table-)cloth

сквозь (+ *A*) through (*esp. of seeing or passing through with difficulty*)

скла́дывать/сложи́ть (**-жу́ -óжишь**) to fold (up); to pack (*one's things, etc.*); to pile (up), heap, stack

сковоро́дка (*G pl.* **-док**) (frying-)pan

ско́лько (+ *G*) how much; how many

ско́лько с меня́? how much/what do I owe?

ско́лько (сейча́с) вре́мени? what's the time (now)?

во ско́лько? (at) what time?

ско́рость *f.* speed, rate, velocity

со ско́ростью 100 киломе́тров в час at a speed of 100 kilometres an hour

ско́рый fast, quick, rapid; forthcoming, near (*in time*)

ско́ро fast, quickly, rapidly; soon, shortly

скоре́е faster, sooner, *etc.*; rather (*more one thing than another*)

скоре́е! quick! hurry up!

скотч sellotape, scotch tape

скри́пка (*G pl.* **-пок**) violin

скро́мный (**-мен -мна́ -мны**) modest, unassuming

скуча́ть (**по** + *D*; *but N.B.* **по нас/вас**) to miss, long for, yearn for (*sb./sth.*)

скуча́ть по до́му to be homesick

я скуча́ю по ним (*D*) I miss them

but **я скуча́ю по вас** (*P*) I miss you

ску́чный (**-чен -чна́ -чны**) boring, dull, tedious, dreary, tiresome

на уро́ке бы́ло ску́чно the lesson was boring

нам ску́чно we're bored

сла́бый (**слаба́**) weak, feeble; faint (*sound*); poor (*health*); bad (*pupil, etc.*)

сла́ва glory, fame, reputation (*see also* **бог**)

сла́вный glorious; fine, good, splendid, nice (*esp. of person*)

сла́дкий (**-док -дка́ -дки**; *comp.* **сла́ще**) sweet

сла́дкое (**-ого**) sweet (course), dessert

сле́ва to/on/from the left (side)

сле́ва от меня́ on my left

сле́довать/по- (**сле́дую -ешь**) (**за** + *I*) to follow, go/come after (*sb./sth.*); (+ *D*) to follow (*example, fashion, etc.*), take after (*sb.*)

как сле́дует properly, as one

should, as it should be, well and truly

сле́дующий following, next (*in order*)

на сле́дующий день (on the) next day

слеза́ (*pl.* **слёзы слёз -а́м**) tear (*that is shed*)

слепо́й (**слеп слепа́ слѐпы**) blind; (*as nn.*) blind man, *etc.*

сли́ва plum

сли́вки (**-вок**) cream

сли́шком too (+ *adj. or adv.*)

слова́рь *m.* (**-аря́**) dictionary, vocabulary

сло́во (*pl.* **-а́**) word

сло́жный complicated, complex, involved, elaborate

слон (**слона́**) elephant

слу́жба (*use* **на**) service, employment, business, work (*esp. military, public, official*)

служи́ть (**-жу́ слу́жишь**) to serve (*in army, etc.*) be employed, work (*in bank, as secretary, etc.*)

слу́чай case, circumstance; chance, opportunity, occasion; event, incident, occurrence

во вся́ком слу́чае in any case, at all events, anyway, anyhow

несча́стный слу́чай accident, mishap

случа́йно by chance/accident, accidentally; by any chance

случа́ться/-чи́ться to happen, occur, come about

что случи́лось? what has

happened? what's up/the matter?

слу́шать/по- (+ *A*) to listen, listen to, hear (*sb./sth.*); to attend (*lectures*)

слу́шать ра́дио to listen to the radio

(**я**) **слу́шаю** hallo; yes? (*on the telephone*)

ты слу́шаешь? are you there? (*on telephone*)

слу́шаю! at your service; very well; yes, sir/madam

слу́шаться/по- (+ *A*) to obey, heed, listen to (*sb.*)

слы́шать/у- (**слы́шу -ишь**) to hear

слы́шно one can hear

(**мне**) **не слы́шно тебя́** I can't hear you

сме́лый (**смела́**) bold, daring, audacious; brave, courageous, fearless

смерть *f.* death

смета́на sour cream

смех laughter, laugh

смешно́й (**смешо́н -шна́ -ы́**) funny, ridiculous, ludicrous, absurd

смешно́ it is funny/makes one laugh

нам не смешно́ we are not amused/don't find it funny

смея́ться/за- (**смею́сь смеёшься**) (+ *D*/**над** + *I*) to laugh (at *sth., e.g. a joke*)/to laugh at, mock, make fun of, deride (*sb./ sth.*)

pf. **рассмея́ться**, *etc.* to burst out laughing

смотре́ть/по- (**смотрю́ смо́тришь**) (**на** + *A*) to look, stare, gaze (at *sb./sth.*); (+ *A*) to watch, see (*film, television, etc.*)

смотре́ть в окно́ to look out of/through the window

смотри́те, не опозда́йте! mind you're not late

посмо́трим we'll see; let me/us see

смысл sense, meaning, point

снача́ла from/at the beginning; (all) over again; at first, first(ly)

снег (**в/на снегу́**) snow

снег идёт it is snowing

снима́ть/снять (**сниму́ сни́мешь**; **сняла́**) to take off (*clothes, record, etc.*); to take a snap/picture/photo (of *sth./sb.*)

сни́мок (**сни́мка**) snap(shot), picture, photograph

сни́ться/при- to dream (*used as below*)

мне присни́лся стра́нный сон I had a strange dream

мне сни́лось, что ... I dreamt that ...

сно́ва *or* **вновь** again, anew, afresh

соба́ка dog

собира́ть/собра́ть (**соберу́ -рёшь**; **собрала́**) to collect, pick, gather (*trans.*)

собира́ться, *etc., but* **собрали́сь** to get/come together, collect, gather, assemble (*intrans.*); to decide, make up one's mind, intend, be going/about to (*do sth.*), be on the point of (*doing sth.*)

собо́р cathedral

собра́ние (*use* **на**) meeting, gathering, assembly (*of organization, group*)

со́бственный (one's) own

собы́тие event, occurrence

соверше́нно completely, absolutely, totally, utterly, perfectly

ты соверше́нно прав you are quite right

сове́т advice, counsel; council, soviet

Верхо́вный Сове́т СССР Supreme Soviet of the USSR

сове́товать/по- (**сове́тую -ешь**) (+ *D* + *inf.*) to advise, recommend (*sb. to do sth.*)

сове́тский Soviet (*adj.*)

Сове́тский Сою́з the Soviet Union

совреме́нный contemporary, modern, present-day, up-to-date

совсе́м quite, entirely

совсе́м не not at all, not a bit, not in the least

согла́сен/-сна/-сны in agreement, agreed

я (не) согла́сен с ней I (dis)agree with her

согла́сны? do you agree? agreed?

соглаша́ться/-си́ться (**соглашу́сь**

-си́шься) to agree, consent, concur

Соединённые Шта́ты Аме́рики (США) the United States of America (USA)

сожале́ние regret

к сожале́нию unfortunately, to one's regret

создава́ть/созда́ть (соз- + дава́ть/дать *but* **со́зда́л(и) -а́)** to create, found; to provide (*conditions, etc.*)

сок juice

солда́т (*G pl.* **солда́т**) soldier, serviceman

со́лнечный sun (*adj.*), solar; sunny

со́лнце sun

сиде́ть на со́лнце to sit in the sun(shine)

соль *f.* salt

сомне́ние doubt

без сомне́ния doubtless, without (any) doubt, undoubtedly

сон (сна; во сне́) sleep; dream (*in sleep*)

ви́деть во сне́ (+ *A*) to dream of/about (*sth./sb.*)

соревнова́ние competition, contest, event (*sporting*)

соревнова́ния по атле́тике athletics meeting, athletic sports (day)

со́рок (*GDIP* **сорока́**) forty

сороково́й fortieth

сорт (*pl.* **-а́ -о́в**) sort, kind; variety, brand; grade, quality

пе́рвого со́рта first-rate

сосе́д (*pl.* **сосе́ди -ей**)/**-ка** (*G pl.* **-док**) neighbour, person next door (*male/female*)

сосе́дний neighbouring, next (-door), adjacent, adjoining

соси́ска (*G pl.* **-сок**) sausage (*individual varieties, frankfurter, etc.*)

сосна́ (*pl.* **со́сны со́сен**) pine (-tree)

состоя́ние condition, state

быть в состоя́нии (+ *inf.*) to be in a position/able (*to do sth.*)

состоя́ть *impf.* (**состои́т**) (**из +** *G*) to consist, be made up (of)

состоя́ться *pf.* (**состои́тся**) to take place (*of organized activities*)

со́тый hundredth

социалисти́ческий socialist

сочине́ние work (*of literature*); essay, composition

сою́з union, alliance

Сою́з Сове́тских Социалисти́ческих Респу́блик (СССР) the Union of Soviet Socialist Republics (USSR)

спа́льня (*G pl.* **спа́лен**) bedroom

спаса́ть/спасти́ (спасу́ -ёшь; спас спасла́) to save, rescue

спаси́бо thank you, thanks

большо́е (вам) спаси́бо thank you very much, many thanks

спать (сплю спишь; спала́) to sleep, be asleep

не спать to be awake

порá (идти́) спать it is time for/ to go to bed, it is bedtime

спектáкль *m.* (*use* **на**) (stage) show, play (*as a spectacle*)

специáльный special, specialized

спеши́ть/по- to hurry (up), be in a hurry, hasten, make haste, get a move on

не спешá without hurrying, in a leisurely way

спинá (**спи́ну -ы́**) back (*of body*)

спи́сок (**спи́ска**; *use* **в**) list

спи́чка (*G pl.* **-чек**) match (*for lighting sth.*)

спокóйный (**-óен -óйна**) calm, tranquil, serene, peaceful, still, quiet, placid

спокóйной нóчи! good night

спóрить/по- (**о** + *P*) to argue, dispute, have an argument/ dispute; to debate, discuss ((about) *sth./sb.*)

спорт (*no pl.*) sport

вы занимáетесь спóртом? do you play/go in for (any) sport(s)?

каки́е ви́ды спóрта вас интересýют? which sports are you interested in?

спорти́вный sporting, athletic, sports (*adj.*)

спорти́вный зал gymnasium, gym

спортсмéн/-ка (*G pl.* **-нок**) sportsman/-woman, athlete

спосóбный (**-бен -бна**) (**к** + *D*) capable, able, gifted, talented, clever, good (at/in *sth.*)

спрáва to/on/from the right (side)

спрáва от меня́ on my right

(**спрáвка**: *see* **медици́нский**)

(**спрáвочный**: *see* **бюрó**)

справедли́вый just, fair

спрáшивать/спроси́ть (**спрошý -óсишь**) (+ *A* /**у** + *G* + **о** + *P*) to ask, enquire (of), question (*sb.* about/after *sth./ sb.*); to ask for, want (to see), wish to speak to (*sb.*)

спускáться/-сти́ться (**спущýсь -ýстишься**) to descend, go/ come down

спускáться на ли́фте to go down in the lift/elevator, take the lift/elevator (down)

спустя́ after, later (*as below*)

немнóго спустя́ a little later, not long after(wards)

спустя́ недéлю a week later

спýтник satellite, sputnik

срáзу at once, immediately, straightaway

средá (**срéду -ы́**; *pl.* **срéды сред -áм**) Wednesday

среди́ (+ *G*) in the middle/midst (of), among

Средизéмное мóре the Mediterranean (Sea)

срéдний middle, medium, average

срéдняя шкóла secondary/ high school

в срéднем on average

ссóриться/по- to quarrel, fall out

(**СССР**: *see* **Сою́з**)

стáвить/по- (**стáвлю -вишь**) to stand, put, place (*sth. in a standing position*); to put on, play (*record*); to park (*car*)

65

стадио́н (*use* **на**) stadium, (*football, etc.*) ground

стака́н glass (*tumbler*)

станови́ться (**-влю́сь -о́вишься**)/ **стать** (**ста́ну -ешь**) to stand (*with motion*), take up a position; (+ *I*) to become, get, turn, grow (*sth., e.g. as below*); (*pf. only*, + *impf. inf.*) to start, begin (*doing sth.*)

   стать на коле́ни to kneel (down)

   стать в о́чередь to (join a) queue

   стать учи́телем to become a teacher

   стано́вится тепле́е/холодне́е it is getting warmer/colder

   ста́ло темно́ it became dark

   что с ней ста́ло? what happened to/has become of her?

стано́к (**станка́**) lathe, bench, machine-tool, machine (*in factory*)

ста́нция (*use* **на**) station

стара́ться/по- to try, endeavour, seek (*to do sth.*)

стари́к (**-а́**) old man

стари́нный ancient, old, antique

ста́роста *m. or f.* prefect, monitor, form rep(resentative), senior pupil/student, group-leader

стару́ха *or* **стару́шка** (*G pl.* **-шек**) old woman, (little) old lady

ста́рый (**стара́**; *comps* **старе́е/ ста́рше; ста́рший**) old (*comps* older *of things/people*)

ста́рший oldest, eldest; elder; senior, head, chief, (person) in charge (*adj. and nn.*)

(**стать:** *see* **станови́ться**)

статья́ (*G pl.* **стате́й**) article (*piece of writing*)

стекло́ (*pl.* **стёкла -кол**) glass (*material*); (window-)pane; windscreen, (*Amer.*) windshield

стена́ (**сте́ну -ы́**; *pl.* **сте́ны стен сте́нам**) wall

сте́пень *f.* (*pl.* **-и -е́й**) degree (*extent or diploma*)

степь *f.* (**в степи́**; *pl.* **-и -е́й**) steppe, plain (*esp. in the USSR*)

стереофони́ческий stereophonic

стипе́ндия grant, bursary, scholarship

стира́льная маши́на washing-machine, washer

стира́ть/вы- *and* **стере́ть** (**сотру́ -ёшь; стёр стёрла**) (*1st pf.*) to wash, launder (*clothes*); (*2nd pf.*) to erase, clean, rub (off), wipe (off)

   стира́ть бельё to do the washing/laundry

стихи́ (**-о́в**) poetry, verse(s)

стихотворе́ние poem

сто (*GDIP* **ста**; *G pl.* **сот**) a hundred

сто́ить to cost, be, come to (*of prices*); to be worth

   ско́лько сто́ит? how much is it/ does it cost?

   ско́лько сто́ят э́ти брю́ки?

how much are these trousers/
do these trousers cost?

стол (стола́; *use* **со)** table; desk,
bureau

сто́лик table (*small, e.g. in a
restaurant*)

столи́ца capital (city)

столо́вая (-ой) dining-room;
(*works, etc.*) canteen, cafeteria,
restaurant

сто́лько (+ *G*) so much, such a
lot; so many

сто́лько ... ско́лько ... as/so
much/many ... as ...

сторона́ (сто́рону -ы́; *pl.*
сто́роны -о́н -а́м) side (*one
as opposed to another*)

перейти́ на другу́ю сто́рону
to go to the other side, cross
over

с пра́вой/ле́вой стороны́ on
the right(-hand)/left(-hand)
side

идти́ в ра́зные сто́роны
to go in various/different
directions

**с одно́й стороны́ ... с друго́й
стороны́** on the one hand ...
on the other hand

стоя́нка parking

ме́сто стоя́нки parking place/
space

стоя́нка маши́н car park,
(*Amer.*) parking lot

стоя́нка такси́ taxi-stand/-
rank, cab-rank

стоя́ть (стою́ -и́шь) to stand, be
standing (up); to be (*in a
standing position, e.g. of bottles*

on a table*), be situated (*of
house, etc.*); be parked (*of
vehicle*)

стои́т си́льный моро́з there is
a hard frost, it is freezing cold/
hard

стоя́ть на коле́нях to kneel (*be
in a kneeling position*)

стой(те)! halt! stop!

страна́ (*pl.* **стра́ны)** country, land
(*nation*)

страни́ца page

**на страни́це сто три́дцать
шесть** *or* **шесто́й (на стр.
136)** on p. 136

стра́нный (-нен -нна́ -нны)
strange, queer, curious, odd,
funny, peculiar

страх fear, fright, dread, terror

стра́шный (-шен -шна́ -шны)
terrible, frightful, fearful,
awful, dreadful, terrifying,
frightening

стреля́ть/вы́стрелить (в + A) to
shoot, fire (*at sth./sb.*)

стро́гий (*adv.* **стро́го;** *comp.*
стро́же) strict, stern, severe

строи́тель *m.* builder

стро́ить/по- to build, construct

**стро́йный (стро́ен, стройна́
-ны)** slim, slender, shapely,
well-proportioned, having a
good figure

студе́нт/-ка (*G pl.* **-ток)** student
(*male/female*)

студе́нческий student (*adj.*)

студе́нческий биле́т *or*
студбиле́т student pass/ID
card

Vocabulary

стул (*pl.* **сту́лья -ьев**; *use* **со**) chair

стуча́ть/по- (**стучу́ -и́шь**) (**в +** *A*) to knock (on/at *sth., e.g. door*)

сты́дно it is shameful
мне сты́дно I am/feel ashamed
как (тебе́ не) сты́дно! for shame! you ought to be ashamed (of yourself)

стюарде́сса stewardess, (air) hostess, flight attendant

суббо́та Saturday

сувени́р souvenir, present, gift (*memento of a trip, etc.*)

судьба́ fate, destiny, lot, fortune

су́мка (*G pl.* **су́мок**) bag (*for shopping, carrying books, etc.*)

су́мма sum, amount (*of money*)

су́мочка (*G pl.* **-чек**) handbag, (*Amer.*) purse

суп soup
суп с мя́сом/ку́рицей meat/chicken soup
суп из овоще́й vegetable soup

су́тки (**су́ток**) 24 hours
кру́глые су́тки round the clock

сухо́й (**сух суха́ су́хи**; *comp.* **су́ше**) dry; dried (*fruit, etc.*)
су́хо it is dry (*not raining*)

существова́ть (**-тву́ю -ешь**) to exist, be (in existence)

(**схвати́ть**: *see* **хвата́ть**)

сходи́ть (**схожу́ -о́дишь**)/**сойти́** (**сойду́ -дёшь; сошёл -шла́**) (**с +** *G*) to go/come/walk down, descend (*sth., from sth. under own power*); to get off/down, alight (*from a vehicle*)

сце́на stage, scene

счастли́вый (**сча́стлив**) happy; fortunate, lucky, successful
счастли́во (остава́ться)! good luck! cheers! look after yourself! (*when saying goodbye*)

сча́стье happiness; good fortune, luck
к сча́стью happily, fortunately, luckily

счёт (*pl.* **счета́ -о́в**) bill, account, (*Amer.*) check, tab; score (*result*)

счита́ть (**+** *A* **+** *I*) to consider, think, reckon, regard (*sb. as sth.*)
я счита́ю его́ свои́м дру́гом I consider him my friend
он счита́ется мои́м дру́гом he is regarded as my friend

(**США**: *see* **Соединённые**)

съезд (*use* **на**) congress, conference, convention

(**съесть**: *see* **есть** 2)

сын (*pl.* **сыновья́ -ве́й -вья́м**) son

сыр (*pl.* **-ы́ -о́в**) cheese

сыро́й damp, soggy, moist; raw, uncooked, unboiled
сы́ро it is damp

сюда́ here (*hither*), this way

сюрпри́з surprise (*event, gift, etc.*)

табле́тка (*G pl.* **-ток**) tablet (*aspirin, etc.*)

тайга́ taiga (*coniferous forest belt in the northern USSR*)

Vocabulary

так thus, like this/that, this/that way; so (+ *adv. or short adj.*)

так же ... как as ... as

так же, как in the same way as, just like

(не) так ли? is(n't) that so/right?

та́к себе so-so, middling, could be worse

так как since, as (*conj.*)

та́кже also, too, as well (*in addition*; tends to stress the whole clause; *cf.* **то́же**)

я та́кже говорю́ по-францу́зски I also speak French (*i.e. French as well*)

та́кже не not either

тако́й such, that kind/sort of; so (+ *long adj.*)

тако́й же ... как as ... as, the same ... as

кто́ она́ така́я? who is she?

что́ э́то тако́е? what is this/that?

что́ тако́е? what's the matter/up? what's that? what did you say?

что́ тако́е `поп-му́зыка`? what is 'pop music'?

такси́ *n. indecl.* (*use* **на**) taxi, cab

тала́нт (**к** + *D*) talent, gift (for *sth.*)

тала́нтливый talented, gifted

там there (*in that place*)

там, где (in the place) where

тамо́жня customs (*custom-house*)

танцева́ть (**-цу́ю -ешь**) to dance

та́нцы (**-цев**) (*use* **на**) dancing, dances; a dance (*ball*)

таре́лка (*G pl.* **-лок**) plate

та́ять/рас- (**та́ет**) to thaw, melt (*intrans.*)

твёрдый (**тверда́**) hard, firm, solid, strong

твой* your; yours (*relates to* **ты**)

теа́тр theatre

текст text

телеви́дение television, TV

по телеви́дению on television (*more official than below*)

телеви́зор television(-set)

смотре́ть переда́чу по телеви́зору to watch a programme on TV (*more coll. than above*)

телегра́мма telegram, cable, wire

дать/посла́ть телегра́мму to send a telegram, to cable, *etc.*

телефо́н (tele)phone

но́мер телефо́на (tele)phone number

кто у телефо́на? who is speaking/who is it (on the phone)?

по телефо́ну on/over the phone

телефо́н-автома́т public telephone, call-box, payphone

те́ло (*pl.* **-а́**) body

тем so much the (+ *comp.*)

тем лу́чше so much the better

те́ма theme, topic, subject

тёмно- dark, deep (*added to adjs. of colour*)

тёмный (**тёмен темна́ -ы́**) dark

на у́лице темно́ it is dark (outside)

температу́ра temperature

те́ннис (lawn) tennis

тень *f.* **(в тени́;** *pl.* **-и -е́й)** shade, shadow

тепе́рь now, at present, nowadays, today

тёплый (*adv.* **тепло́**) warm, mild; cordial

  сего́дня тепло́ it is warm/mild today

  тебе́ тепло́? are you warm?

терпе́ние patience, endurance, perseverance

терпе́ть/по- (**терплю́ те́рпишь**) to suffer, undergo, sustain, endure; to bear, put up with, stand, tolerate; to experience, have (*accident, etc.*)

теря́ть/по- to lose (*no longer have sth.*)

  теря́ться/по- to get lost, be lost, lose one's way; to lose one's head/presence of mind, be(come) embarrassed

тетра́дка (*G pl.* **-док**) *or* **тетра́дь** *f.* exercise book, notebook

тётя (*G pl.* **тётей**) aunt

те́хника engineering, technology

те́хникум technical school/college

течь (**течёт теку́т; тёк текла́**) to flow, stream, run (*of liquids*); to pass, go by (*of time*)

тигр tiger

ти́хий (**тиха́;** *сотр.* **ти́ше**) quiet, silent, soundless, noiseless, faint, gentle, soft, low (*of sounds*), calm, serene, peaceful, still

  ти́ше! (be) quiet! silence! hush! gently (does it)! go easy!

Ти́хий океа́н the Pacific (Ocean)

тишина́ quiet, silence, peace(fulness), stillness

то then (*following an 'if' clause*)

-то/-нибудь (*added to e.g.* **где-, как-, како́й-, когда́-, кто-, куда́-, почему́-, чей-, что-,** *as below*) some-/any-, some- or other (*def. but not identified/indef., implying choice or doubt, used in questions, fut., etc.*)

где́-то somewhere, (at) some place

где́-нибудь somewhere (or other), at some place or other

ка́к-то somehow

ка́к-нибудь somehow, in some way or other

како́й-то some (*adj.*)

како́й-нибудь some or other, any (*adj.*), a

когда́-то at one time, once, some time ago

когда́-нибудь some day, ever, at one time (or other)

кто́-то someone, somebody

кто́-нибудь anyone, anybody, somebody or other

куда́-то somewhere, (to) some place

куда́-нибудь somewhere (or other), anywhere

почему́-то for some reason

чей-то (*see* **чей***) somebody's, someone (else)'s

что́-то something

что́-нибудь something or other

това́рищ (*G pl.* **-щей;** *sometimes*

written **тов.** *or* **т.**) comrade;
colleague, companion, friend,
mate; chum, pal, buddy; (*of
Soviet citizens or socialists
elsewhere*) Mr, Mrs, Miss, Ms;
a person, gentleman, man, lady
(*used politely in 3rd pers.*)
шко́льный това́рищ school
friend
това́рищ по кла́ссу classmate
това́рищ по рабо́те workmate,
fellow-worker, colleague (at
work)
това́рищи! comrades! (ladies
and) gentlemen!
тогда́ then, at that time; in that
case
то́ есть (т.е.) that is (to say), i.e.
то́же also, too, as well (*similarly;
tends to stress the subject*; *cf.*
та́кже)
**я то́же говорю́ по-
францу́зски** I also speak
French (*i.e. I too*)
то́же не not either
у нас то́же нет neither/nor
have we
Ты уста́л? Я то́же. Are you
tired? So am I/Me, too.
Ты не уста́л? Я то́же. You're
not tired? Nor am I.
толка́ть/-кну́ть (-ну́ -нёшь) to
push, shove, nudge, jog
толпа́ (*pl.* **то́лпы**) crowd, throng
то́лстый (толста́; *comp.* **то́лще)**
thick, heavy; fat, stout,
corpulent
то́лько only, merely, solely, just;
but (at the same time)

не то́лько ... но и ... not only
... but (also)
как то́лько as soon as, the
moment ...
то́лько что (only) just, just now
(**тому́ наза́д:** *see* **наза́д**)
то́нкий (то́нок -нка́ -нки; *comp.*
то́ньше) thin, slim, slender;
delicate, fine, subtle
тону́ть/по- *and* **у- (тону́
то́нешь)** (*1st pf.*) to sink, go
down (*of boats*); (*2nd pf.*) to
drown, be drowned
торго́вля (*no pl.*) trade,
commerce, business
торго́вый центр shopping
centre/precinct/mall
торт cake (*of gâteau type*)
тост toast (*piece of toasted bread*)
тот/та/то/те* that (pl. those); the
other (*side, etc.*); that one (*pl.*
those (ones), *pron.*)
тот/не тот the right/the wrong
то́т же (са́мый) the (very) same
э́то совсе́м не то́ it isn't that at
all, that's quite wrong
то́чка (*G pl.* **-чек**) point, dot,
spot; full stop, (*Amer.*) period
то́чный (-чен -чна́ -чны) exact,
precise, accurate, faithful;
punctual
то́чно exactly, *etc.*; on the dot,
sharp (*at a time*); right, just
(*precisely*)
тошни́ть (*used as below*)
меня́, *etc.*, **тошни́т** I, *etc.*, feel
sick
трава́ (*pl.* **тра́вы**) grass; herb
тра́ктор tractor

трамва́й (*use* **на** *or* **в**) tram, (*Amer.*) streetcar

транзи́стор transistor (radio)

тра́тить/ис- *and* **по-** (**тра́чу тра́тишь**) to spend, expend, use up (*and often* waste; *of money, time, strength, etc.*)

тре́бовать/по- (**-бую -ешь**) (+ *G*) to demand, require, call for

тре́тий* third

    тре́тье (-ьего) *nn.* third course (*of meal*), dessert, sweet, afters, pudding (course)

три (**трёх трём тремя́ трёх**) three

тридца́тый thirtieth

три́дцать (-ати́) thirty

трина́дцатый thirteenth

трина́дцать thirteen

три́ста (**трёхсо́т трёмста́м**, *etc.*) three hundred

тро́гать/тро́нуть (-ну -нешь) to touch; to move (*emotionally*)

    не тро́гай (тронь) меня́! leave me alone!

тро́е (**трои́х**, *etc., but usu. replaced by* **трёх**, *etc.*) three (*used esp. where G pl. is lexically obligatory*)

    их бы́ло тро́е there were three of them

    тро́е сане́й three sledges

тро́йка (*G pl.* **тро́ек**) a three, average/fair/satisfactory mark, C (*in Soviet 5-point system*); troika (*Russian three-horse carriage or sleigh*)

тролле́йбус (*use* **на** *or* **в**) trolley(bus)

тролле́йбусом by trolley

тротуа́р pavement, footpath, (*Amer.*) sidewalk

тру́бка (*G pl.* **-бок**) (telephone) receiver; (tobacco-)pipe

труд (труда́) labour, toil, (hard) work; trouble, difficulty

    с трудо́м with difficulty, hardly

    без труда́ without difficulty, without (any) effort

тру́дный (**-ден -дна́ -дны**) hard, difficult, arduous

    тру́дно it is hard, *etc.*

    мне тру́дно говори́ть по-неме́цки I find it hard to speak German

тру́сики (-ов) shorts; (swimming) trunks; (under)pants

туале́т *or* **убо́рная (-ой)** lavatory, WC, toilet, loo, public convenience

    мужско́й туале́т Gentlemen, Gents

    да́мский туале́т Ladies

туда́ there (*thither*), that way

    не туда́ the wrong way, in the wrong direction, not that way

    биле́т туда́ и обра́тно a return/round-trip ticket

тума́н mist, fog, haze

    на у́лице тума́н it is misty/foggy (outside)

ту́ндра tundra (*treeless subarctic plain in the USSR*)

тури́ст/-ка (*G pl.* **-ток**) tourist; hiker, tramper, trekker,

Vocabulary

backpacker; hosteller, camper (*male/female*)
туристский traveller's, tourist's, tourist (*adj.*)
тут here (*in this place*)
туфли (**туфель**; *s.* **-ля**) shoes
домашние туфли slippers
туча (dark/black/rain/storm-)cloud
ты (**тебя тебе тобой тебе**) you (*thou*)
я с ней на ты I am on familiar terms with her, she and I are close
тысяча a thousand
тюрьма (*pl.* **тюрьмы тюрем**) prison, jail (gaol)
тяжёлый (**тяжела -ы**) heavy; severe, painful, distressing, serious, bad (*illness, etc.*); laborious, strenuous, difficult, hard (*task, work, etc.*); close, oppressive (*of weather*)
тяжело heavily, *etc.*; it is hard, *etc.*
мне тяжело it is hard/painful, *etc.*, for me; I feel miserable/wretched/rotten
тянуть/по- (**-у тянешь**) to pull, drag, draw, haul

у (**+ G**) by, at (*beside*); with (*at the house of*); from (*of buying, taking sth. from sb.*); (*see also* **быть**)
у врача at the doctor's
у себя at one's own place; at home, in
убегать/-жать (**убегу -жишь**

-гут) to run away, run/make off; to escape
убеждать/убедить (*no 1st pers. s. fut.*) (*A* + **в** + *P*; *A* + *inf.*) to convince, persuade (*sb.* of *sth.*, to do *sth.*; *impf. may have sense* to try to . . .)
убеждаться, *etc.* (**в** + *P*) to become/be persuaded (of *sth.*), to make sure/certain, satisfy oneself (of *sth.*)
убивать/убить (**убью -ёшь**; *imp.* **убей(те)**)) to kill, murder, assassinate
убирать/убрать (**уберу -ёшь**; **убрала**) to take away, remove; to put away, clear; to tidy (up), make (up), do (*room, bed*); to gather/bring in, reap, harvest (*crops*)
убирать со стола to clear the table, clear up/away
(**уборная**: *see* **туалет**)
уверен/-а/-ы (**в** + *P*; **что**) sure, certain, confident (of *sth.*; that . . .)
угодно (*used as below*)
что вам угодно? what can I do for you? what would you like?
как (вам) угодно as you please/wish, please yourself
сколько угодно (**+ G**) as much as you like/want, any amount (*of sth.*)
угол (**угла**) corner; angle
в/на углу in/at/on the corner
за углом round the corner
из-за угла (from) round the corner

у́голь *m.* (**у́гля́**) coal

удава́ться (**удаётся**)/**уда́ться** (**уда́стся удаду́тся; уда́лся уда́ла́сь -и́сь**) to succeed, be a success/successful, turn out well, work (well)

мне, *etc.*, **удало́сь** (+ *inf.*) I, *etc.*, managed (*to do sth.*), succeeded (*in doing sth.*)

мне не удало́сь I did not manage, I failed

ударя́ть/уда́рить (+ *A* + **по** + *D*) to hit, strike, slap, knock, punch (*sb. on part of body*)

ударя́ть ного́й (*e.g.* **в дверь**) to kick (*e.g.* at/on the door)

ударя́ться, *etc.* (+ *I* + **о** + *A*) to hit, strike, knock (*some part of one's body* on sth.)

удиви́тельный (**-лен -льна**) surprising, astonishing, amazing, wonderful, marvellous

удивле́ние surprise, astonishment, amazement, wonder

удивля́ть/-ви́ть (**удивлю́ -ви́шь**) to surprise, astonish, amaze

удивля́ться, *etc.* (+ *D*) to be surprised/astonished/amazed (by/at *sth.*), to wonder, marvel (at *sth.*)

удо́бный (**-бен -бна**) comfortable, cosy; suitable, convenient, opportune

мне, *etc.*, **удо́бно** I, *etc.*, am/feel comfortable/at my ease; it is convenient for/suits me

удово́льствие pleasure, delight, enjoyment

с удово́льствием gladly, by all means, with pleasure

уезжа́ть/уе́хать (**уе́ду -ешь**) (**из/ с/от** + *G*) to go (away), leave, depart (from *a place*; *not on foot*)

они́ уе́хали (**отсю́да**) they have left (here)/are away

уж (*emphatic particle, used as below*)

уж я не зна́ю I really don't know, I'm sure I don't know

ты уж не говори́! don't you go and tell

э́то не так уж легко́ that's not so (very) easy

ужа́сный (**-сен -сна**) awful, dreadful, horrible, terrible, frightful, ghastly

уже́ already, (by) now, by this time

уже́ не(т) no longer, not any more

у́жин supper *or* evening meal, tea, dinner (*when* **обе́д** *is used of the midday meal*)

у́жинать/по- to have (one's) supper *or* to have one's evening meal/tea/dinner

у́зкий (**у́зок узка́ у́зко у́зки́**; *comp.* **у́же**) narrow; tight (*of clothes, shoes*); (*with end stress in n. and pl. short forms*) too tight

узнава́ть (**-наю́ -ёшь**)/**узна́ть** (+ *A*) to recognize; to learn, find out, get to know (of/about), to become familiar with

ука́зывать/указа́ть (**укажу́ -а́жешь**) (+ *A*) to show, indicate, point (out), explain (*the way, etc.*); (**на** + *A*) to point (at/to *sth.*), point out (*mistakes, etc.*)

Украи́на (*use* **на**) the Ukraine

у́лица street

жить на у́лице Турге́нева to live in/on Turgenev Street

на у́лице тепло́ it is warm out(side)

вы́йти на у́лицу to go out(side)

улучше́ние improvement, amelioration

улыба́ться/улыбну́ться (-у́сь -ёшься) (+ *D*) to smile (*at sb.*)

улы́бка (*G pl.* **-бок**) smile

ум (ума́) mind, intellect, intelligence

мне пришло́ на ум it occurred to me

сойти́ с ума́ to go mad

уме́ть/с- (+ *inf.*) to know how to, be able to, can (*read, swim, etc.; in pf. also* to manage to, succeed in *doing sth.*)

умира́ть/умере́ть (умру́ -рёшь; у́мер(ли) умерла́) to die, pass away (*pf. also* to be dead)

они́ у́мерли they are dead/ (have) died

умере́ть от гри́ппа to die of/ from influenza

у́мный (умён умна́ у́мны) clever, intelligent, wise, sensible

умыва́ться/умы́ться (умо́юсь -ешься) to wash (one's hands and face), have a wash, get washed

универма́г department store

универса́м supermarket, self-service store

университе́т university, (*Amer.*) school

уноси́ть (уношу́ -о́сишь)/унести́ (унесу́ -сёшь; унёс унесла́) to carry/take (away *with one*)

(упа́сть: *see* **па́дать)**

употребля́ть/-би́ть (-блю́ -би́шь) to use, make use of, employ

упражне́ние exercise

ура́! hooray! hoorah! hurrah!

Ура́л (*use* **на**) the Urals

урожа́й harvest, crop

уро́к (*use* **на**) lesson, period (*in school day*); homework (*for a particular lesson*)

уро́к ру́сского языка́ Russian lesson

де́лать/гото́вить уро́ки to do one's homework/prep

усе́рдно enthusiastically, keenly, eagerly, diligently, hard (*of doing one's work, etc.*)

уси́лие effort

усло́вия *n. pl.* (**-ий**) conditions, terms

успева́ть/успе́ть (+ *inf.* /**к** + *D or* **на** + *A*) to have time, manage (*to do sth.*)/to be in time (*for sth., e.g. lunch/train*)

успе́х success

име́ть успе́х to succeed, be successful, go off well

не име́ть успе́ха to fail, be a failure

де́лать успе́хи to make

progress, do/get on well,
advance

желáю вам успéха/-ов I wish
you (every) success/good luck!

**уставáть (устаю́ -ёшь)/устáть
(устáну -ешь) (от + G)** to
get/become tired/weary
(from/with/of *sth.*; *in pf. also
to be tired/weary*)

я устáл I became tired; I am
tired

они́ устáли игрáть they are
tired of playing

устáлый (*no short forms*) tired,
weary

устрáивать/устрóить to arrange,
organize

усы́ (усóв) moustache

у́тка (*G pl.* **у́ток**) duck

у́тренний morning (*adj.*)

у́тро (*stress regular except as
below*) morning

4 часá/5, 6, ... 11 часóв утрá
4/5, 6, ... 11 a.m.

на (слéдующее) у́тро next
morning, in the morning (*of the
next day*)

у́тром in the morning (*of any
day*)

в понедéльник у́тром on
Monday morning

по утрáм in the mornings

до утрá until morning

с утрá до вéчера from morning
till night, all day long

утю́г (-á) (*smoothing*) iron

у́хо (*pl.* **у́ши ушéй**) ear

**уходи́ть (ухожу́ -óдишь)/уйти́
(уйду́ -дёшь; ушёл ушлá)**

(из/с/от + G) to go (away/
off), leave, depart (from *a
place*; *under own power*)

**учáствовать (-твую -ешь) (в +
P)** to participate, take part (in
sth.)

учéбник (text)book, course
(-book), manual, primer

учéбный educational, academic,
school (*adj.*)

учени́к (-á)/-и́ца pupil, (*Amer.*)
student (*male/female*)

учёный learned, scholarly;
scientific; (*as nn.*) scholar;
scientist

учи́тель *m.* (*pl.* **-я́ -éй**)**/-ница**
teacher, tutor, schoolteacher,
(school)master/mistress (*cf.*
преподавáтель)

учи́тель матемáтики maths
teacher

**учи́ть/на- and вы́- (учу́ у́чишь)
(+ A + D or + inf.)** (*1st pf.*)
to teach (*sb. sth., to do sth.*);
(*2nd pf.*) to study, learn,
memorize (*lesson, role, etc.*)

**онá у́чит меня́ рýсскому
языкý** she teaches me
Russian

я научи́л егó игрáть в тéннис
I taught him to play tennis

**он ужé вы́учил все нóвые
словá** he has already learnt all
the new words

**учи́ться/на- or вы́- (+ D or
inf.)** to learn (*a subject, to do
sth.*); to study, read (*a subject*);
(*no pf.*) to study, be a student,
be (*at university, school*)

я учу́сь му́зыке I am learning/
studying music
они́ у́чатся в институ́те they
are (studying) at the institute
У́эльс Wales
ую́тный (-тен -тна) cosy, snug,
comfortable

фа́брика (*use* **на**) factory, works,
mill (*mainly in light industries*)
факт fact
факульте́т (*use* **на**) faculty,
(*large*) department, school (*in
higher educational
establishments*)
фами́лия (sur)name, family name
как ва́ша фами́лия? what is
your (sur)name?
(фанта́стика: *see* **нау́чный)**
февра́ль *m.* **(-аля́)** February
фен hair-dryer
фе́рма (*use* **на**) farm (*outside the
Soviet Union or specialized
establishment within*)
фе́рмер farmer (*outside the Soviet
Union*)
фи́зика physics
физкульту́ра physical education/
training, PE, PT, gym(nastics)
(*subject in school, etc.*)
фильм film, picture, movie
флаг flag, colours, ensign
флейта flute, recorder
флот (*use* **во**) fleet, navy
вое́нно-морско́й флот the
Navy
(вое́нно-)возду́шный флот
the Air Force
фонта́н fountain

фо́рма shape, form; uniform
фотоаппара́т camera
**фотографи́ровать/с- (-и́рую
-ешь)** to photograph, take a
photo(graph)/photo(graph)s
(of)
фотографи́роваться, *etc.* to be
photographed, have one's
photo(graph)/picture taken
фотогра́фия photography;
photo(graph), picture
фотоко́пия (photo)copy, xerox,
photostat
снять фотоко́пию (с + *G*) to
take/make a (photo)copy (of
sth.)
Фра́нция (*use* **во**) France
францу́женка (*G pl.* **-нок**)
French(woman)
францу́з French(man) (*pl.* the
French)
францу́зский French (*adj.*; *see
also* **по-**)
фрукто́вый fruit (*adj.*), fruit-
flavoured, soft (*drink*)
фру́кты (-ов; *s.* **фрукт**) fruit
(*collectively*; *s. individual item
of fruit, kind of fruit*)
фунт pound (*weight or money*)
футбо́л (association) football,
soccer

хала́т dressing-gown, bath-robe;
housecoat; overall, smock
хара́ктер character, nature,
disposition, personality
хвали́ть/по- (-лю́ хва́лишь) (+ *A*
+ **за** + *A*) to praise,
compliment (*sb.* for/on *sth.*)

Vocabulary

хвата́ть/схвати́ть (-ачу́ -а́тишь) to seize, snatch, grasp, catch hold of, grab

хвата́ть/хвати́ть (хва́тит) to suffice, be sufficient/enough (*used impersonally as below*)

э́того (нам, *etc.***) хва́тит на неде́лю** this is enough for/will last (us, *etc.*) a week

не хвата́ет вре́мени (+ *inf.***)** there is no time/isn't time (*to do sth.*)

у меня́, *etc.***, не хвата́ет де́нег** I, *etc.*, am short of money

хва́тит! that will do/is enough

хвост (-а́) tail

хи́мия chemistry

хлеб bread; loaf

чёрный хлеб brown bread; rye bread

ходи́ть (хожу́ хо́дишь) (*indef.*) to walk, go, come (*on foot*); to run (*of buses, trains*)

идти́ (иду́ идёшь; шёл шла)/ пойти́ (пойду́; пошёл) (*def.*) to walk, go, come (*on foot*); to go, come, leave, start (*of buses, trains*); to go, work (*of timepiece, machine*); to fall (*of rain, snow*); to pass (*of time passing*); to be on/in progress/ showing (*of event, spectacle*)

ходи́ть в шко́лу to attend school

ходи́ть в шу́бе to wear a fur coat (*habitually*)

пойдём(те) в кино́! let's go to the pictures

идёт! all right, agreed, OK

хозя́ин (*pl.* **хозя́ева -ев**) master; owner, proprietor; boss; landlord; host (*master of house*)

хозя́йка (*G pl.* **-я́ек**) mistress; owner, proprietress; boss; landlady; hostess (*mistress of house*)

хозя́йство economy

се́льское хозя́йство agriculture, farming

(дома́шнее) хозя́йство housekeeping; housework

хокке́й hockey; ice-hockey

холм (-а́) (*low*) hill

холоди́льник refrigerator, fridge, (*Amer.*) ice-box

холо́дный (хо́лоден -дна́ -дны) cold

хо́лодно it is cold

мне, *etc.***, хо́лодно** I, *etc.*, am/ feel cold

хор choir, chorus

хо́ром in chorus, all together

хоро́ший (-ша́ -ши́; *comp.* **лу́чше лу́чший)** good (better, best); fine, nice (*weather*); (*in short forms, usu. with* **собо́й**) good-looking, pretty, attractive

хорошо́/лу́чше well/better (*adv.*)

хорошо́ (+ *inf.***)** it is nice/ pleasant (*to do sth.*)

хорошо́! good, (all) right, very well, fine, agreed, OK

мне лу́чше сего́дня I am/feel better today

нам лу́чше оста́ться здесь we had better stay here

хоте́ть/за- (хочу́ хо́чешь -ет хоти́м -и́те -я́т) to want, wish, desire, (*in cond.*) would like; to mean, intend, be about (*to do sth.*)
   е́сли хоти́те if you wish/like
   как хоти́те as you wish/like
   хоте́ть сказа́ть to mean (to say), try to say
   хоте́ть есть to be hungry
   хоте́ть пить to be thirsty
   хоте́ть спать to be sleepy
   мне, *etc.*, хо́чется есть/пить/спать I, *etc.*, feel hungry/thirsty/sleepy; I, *etc.*, should like to eat/have a drink/go to bed
хоть even if (only), even when, at least
   приходи́ хоть ты *you* come, anyway
хотя́ although, though
хра́брый (храбра́) brave, courageous
худо́жественный artistic, art (*adj.*)
худо́жник artist, painter
(ху́дший, ху́же: *see* плохо́й)

царь *m.* (царя́) tsar, czar (*pre-Revolutionary Russian autocrat*)
цвет (*pl.* -а́ -о́в) colour
   како́го цве́та? what colour?
цветно́й coloured, colour (*adj.*)
цвето́к (цветка́; *pl.* цветы́ -о́в) flower
целова́ть/по- (целу́ю -ешь) (+ A + в + A) to kiss (*trans.*; *sb.'s sth., sb. on the sth.*)
   она́ поцелова́ла его́ в щёку she kissed him on the cheek
   целова́ться, *etc.* to kiss (each other)
це́лый (цела́) intact, unbroken, unhurt, safe, in one piece, whole; (*long forms only*) whole, entire, all
   це́лую неде́лю (for) a whole week
   це́лый день all day long
   це́лых пять лет (for) five whole years, all of five years
цель *f.* aim, purpose, end, object(ive), goal; target
цена́ (це́ну -ы́; *pl.* це́ны) price, cost; value, worth
це́нности (-ей) (one's) valuables, objects of value
це́нный valuable, costly
центр centre; city centre
центра́льный central
це́рковь *f.* (це́ркви -овью; *pl.* це́ркви -ве́й -ва́м) church
цех (work)shop; department (*in factory*)
цирк circus

чай (*G s.* ча́я *or* ча́ю) tea; afternoon tea, tea-party
   ча́шка ча́я/-ю a cup of tea
   за ча́ем during/over tea, at tea-time
   пригласи́ть (+ A) на чай to invite (*sb.*) (round) to tea
   дать (+ D) на чай to tip (*sb.*), give (*sb.*) a tip

79

Vocabulary

ча́йник teapot; (tea-)kettle

час (**ча́са**, *but see below*; *pl.* **-ы́ -о́в**) hour; time (of day)
  че́тверть часа́ a quarter (of an) hour
  кото́рый час? what is the time (of day)? what time is it?
  час/2 часа́, *etc.* one/2 o'clock, *etc.*
  в пе́рвом часу́ after midday/midnight (and before one), between twelve and one
  час обе́да lunchtime, dinnertime, lunch hour/break
  свобо́дные часы́ free time, leisure hours

ча́стный private, personal, privately-owned

ча́сто (*comp.* **ча́ще**) often, frequently
  ча́ще всего́ mostly, most often

часть *f.* (*pl.* **-и -е́й**) part, portion, section; some (*with pl. nn.*)
  бо́льшая часть the greater part, most
  бо́льшей ча́стью for the most part, mostly

часы́ (**-о́в**) clock; watch

ча́шка (*G pl.* **ча́шек**) cup

(**ча́ще**: *see* **ча́сто**)

чей* whose (*chiefly interrog.*)
  чей э́то каранда́ш? whose is this pencil? who does this pencil belong to?

чек cheque, (*Amer.*) check; bill (*to take to cash-desk*); receipt, chit (*given at cash-desk*)
  доро́жный *or* **тури́стский чек** traveller's cheque

челове́к (*pl.* **лю́ди -де́й лю́дям людьми́ лю́дях**; *but G pl.*
  челове́к *after numerals*) man; person (*pl. also* people); human being

чем than

чемода́н (suit)case

чемпио́н champion, title-holder
  чемпио́н по те́ннису tennis champion

че́рез (+ *A*) across, over (*of motion across*); through; via; in, after (*period of time*)
  че́рез час in an hour('s time) *or* every other hour

черни́ла (**-ни́л**) *pl.* ink

Чёрное мо́ре the Black Sea

чёрный black

черта́ line; feature (*of face*); trait, characteristic

че́стный (**-тен -тна́ -тны**) honest

четве́рг (**-а́**) Thursday

четвёрка (*G pl.* **-рок**) a four, good mark, B (*in Soviet 5-point marking system*)

че́тверо (**-ых**, *etc.*, *but usu. replaced by* **четырёх**, *etc.*) four (*used esp. where G pl. is lexically obligatory*)
  че́тверо часо́в four clocks/watches

четвёртый fourth

че́тверть *f.* (*pl.* **-и -е́й**) a quarter, one fourth; term (*in school year*)
  че́тверть пе́рвого, *etc.* a quarter past twelve, *etc.*
  без че́тверти час, *etc.* a quarter to one, *etc.*

четы́ре (четырёх -рём -рьмя́ -рёх) four

четы́реста (четырёхсо́т четырёмста́м, *etc.*) four hundred

четы́рнадцатый fourteenth

четы́рнадцать fourteen

число́ (*pl.* чи́сла чи́сел) number; date

како́е сего́дня число́? what is the date (today)? what date is it (today)?

како́го числа́? (on) what date?

чи́стить/по- (чи́щу чи́стишь) to clean, brush, polish

чи́стый (чиста́; *comp.* чи́ще) clean; pure; clear (*air, etc.*)

чита́ть/про- to read; to recite (*poetry*), to give, deliver (*a lecture*)

член member

что 1 that (*conj.*)

что 2 (чего́ чему́ чем чём) what (*interrog. and rel. pron.*)

что с тобо́й? what's the matter/ up/wrong with you?

что де́лать? what can I, *etc.*, do?

что э́то за пти́ца? what (kind/ sort of) bird is that?

что за пого́да! what weather!

то, что what (*the thing which*)

я говорю́ о том, что я ви́дел I am speaking of what I saw

я зна́ю, что́ вы ви́дели I know what you saw

что́бы (*or* чтоб; *used with inf. or to form subjunct.*) in order to, so as to, to; in order that,

so that, that, (*with neg.*) lest

чувстви́тельный (-лен -льна) sensitive, tender, sentimental

чу́вство feeling, sense

чу́вствовать/по- (чу́вствую -ешь) to feel (*sth., e.g. pain*)

чу́вствовать себя́ лу́чше/ больны́м, *etc.* to feel better/ ill, *etc.*

чуде́сный (-сен -сна) marvellous, wonderful, lovely, splendid

чуде́сно! (how) wonderful! splendid!

чужо́й somebody/someone else's, another person's, other people's

э́то чужи́е кни́ги these aren't my books

в чужо́м до́ме in a strange house

я здесь чужа́я I'm a stranger here

чуло́к (чулка́; *G pl.* чуло́к) stocking (*pl. also* hose)

чуть barely, scarcely, hardly

чуть не almost, very nearly

шаг (ша́га, *but* 2/3/4 шага́; *pl.* -и́ -о́в) pace, step, stride, tread

шампа́нское (-ого) champagne, bubbly, sparkling wine

ша́пка (*G pl.* ша́пок) cap, hat (*esp. of fur, with earflaps*)

шарф scarf, muffler

ша́хматы (-мат) chess

ша́хта mine, pit

шахтёр miner

ша́шки (ша́шек) draughts, (*Amer.*) checkers

шашлы́к (-а́) shashlyk, (shish)kebab (*pieces of meat, onions, etc., grilled on skewer*)

шерстяно́й woollen, wool (*adj.*)

шестидеся́тый sixtieth

шестна́дцатый sixteenth

шестна́дцать sixteen

шесто́й sixth

шесть (шести́) six

шестьдеся́т (шести́десяти) sixty

шестьсо́т (шестисо́т -ста́м) six hundred

ше́я neck

ширина́ width, breadth
   шириной в два ме́тра *or* **два ме́тра в ширину́** two metres wide/in width

широ́кий (широ́к -а́ -и́; *comp.* **ши́ре)** wide, broad; large, big (*in width*); (*in short forms*) too wide, too large, *etc.*
   широко́ widely, wide; extensively

шить/с- (шью шьёшь; *imp.* **шей(те))** to sew; to make (*by sewing*)

шкаф (в/на шкафу́; *pl.* **-ы́ -о́в)** cupboard, dresser, wardrobe, safe, bookcase (*with doors*)

шко́ла school

шко́льник schoolboy (*pl. also* schoolchildren)

шко́льница schoolgirl

шко́льный school (*adj.*)

шля́па hat

шокола́д (*no pl.*) chocolate (*to drink, or to eat in bar form*; *cf.* **конфе́та**)

шоссе́ *n. indecl.* surfaced road; highway, exit road (*main road out of town*)

шотла́ндец (-дца) Scotsman, Scot (*pl.* the Scots/Scottish)

шотла́ндка (*G pl.* **-док)** Scotswoman, Scot

Шотла́ндия Scotland

шотла́ндский Scottish, Scots

шофёр driver; chauffeur (*hired to drive a car*)
   шофёр такси́ taxi-driver, cab-driver

штат state (*federal, e.g. in the USA, Australia*)

шу́ба fur coat

шум noise; sound; racket; row, uproar, din, hubbub, *etc.*; murmur, rustle, *etc.*

шуме́ть (шумлю́ шуми́шь) to make a noise, be noisy; to sound, murmur, *etc.*

шу́мный (-мен -мна́ -мны) noisy, loud

шути́ть/по- (шучу́ шу́тишь) to joke, crack jokes, jest, make funny remarks
   я не шучу́ I'm serious, I mean it

шу́тка (*G pl.* **шу́ток)** joke, jest, funny remark
   в шу́тку as a joke, jokingly, in fun
   не на шу́тку seriously, in earnest

ще́дрый (щедра́) generous, liberal, lavish

щека́ (щёку щеки́; *pl.* щёки щёк
щека́м) cheek (*part of face*)
щено́к (щенка́) puppy
щётка (*G pl.* щёток) brush
щи (щей) schi (*cabbage soup*)

ЭВМ (электро́нно-
вычисли́тельная маши́на)
computer (*mainframe, etc.*)
экза́мен (*use* на) exam(ination),
test
  экза́мен по матема́тике maths
  exam
экску́рсия guided tour, excursion,
outing, sightseeing trip; tour
party/group
экскурсово́д guide, tour-leader
электри́ческий electric, (electric)
power, electrical
электри́чество electricity,
power; (electric) light
электро́ника electronics
электроста́нция (*use* на)
(electric) power-station
  а́томная электроста́нция
  atomic/nuclear power-station
энерги́чный (-чен -чна)
vigorous, energetic, forceful
эскала́тор escalator, moving
staircase
эта́ж (-а́) floor, storey, level
  пе́рвый эта́ж ground floor,
  street level
  второ́й эта́ж, *etc.* first floor,
  level one, *etc.*
э́тот/э́та/э́то/э́ти* this (*pl.* these);
this one (*pl.* these (ones);
pron.)

э́то this, that, it; this/that/it is,
these/those/they are

ю́бка (*G pl.* ю́бок) skirt
юг (*use* на) south
ю́жный south (*adj.*), southern,
southerly
ю́ность *f.* youth (*period of life;
more literary than* мо́лодость)
ю́ноша *m.* (*G. pl.* -ей) youth,
young man (*late teens to early
twenties*)
ю́ный young (*usu. younger or
more literary than* молодо́й;
used e.g. of Pioneers); youthful
юри́ст lawyer, legal expert/
adviser

я (меня́ мне мной мне) I; me,
etc.
я́блоко (*pl.* -ки -ок) apple
явля́ться/яви́ться (явлю́сь
я́вишься) to present oneself,
appear, come, arrive, report,
register, show/turn up; to be
(*in literary or official usage*)
  Москва́ явля́ется столи́цей
  СССР Moscow is the capital
  of the USSR
я́года berry; berry fruit, soft fruit
я́дерный nuclear
язы́к (-а́; *use* на, *but N.B. see* по-)
tongue; language
  гре́ческий/кита́йский, *etc.*,
  язы́к Greek/Chinese
  (language), *etc.*
  говори́ть на трёх языка́х to
  speak three languages
яйцо́ (*pl.* я́йца яи́ц я́йцам) egg

Vocabulary

янва́рь *m.* (**-аря́**) January
япо́нец (**япо́нца**) Japanese (*male*)
япо́нка (*G pl.* **-нок**) Japanese (*female*)
Япо́ния Japan
япо́нский Japanese (*adj.*)
я́ркий (**я́рок ярка́ я́рки**; *comp.* **я́рче**) bright, shining, brilliant, glaring, blazing, striking, vivid, colourful, graphic

я́рко- bright (*added to adjs of colour*)
я́сли (**я́слей**; *no s.*) crèche, (day) nursery
я́сный (**я́сен ясна́ я́сны**) clear, fine, lucid, distinct
я́сно clearly, *etc.*; it is clear/fine; that is clear, yes, I see, *etc.*
я́щик box, case, bin, chest; drawer (*see also* **почто́вый**)

REPEAT LIST OF MOST BASIC WORDS

Note

1   As with the entire Vocabulary, selection here has been to some extent arbitrary. The intention is to provide for an average cross-section of needs, but everything will depend on the contexts in which the words are to be used. Names of sports, for instance, must be added where they are considered important, as also further words for clothing, food and drink. Those students whose home is not Britain or the United States will need relevant nationality terms. The list should be treated as a useful base, not as a canon of law.

2   Asterisks again indicate that the declension of words so marked must be looked up in a grammar book. *All* words here included must, of course, be checked in the main Vocabulary for definition and usage, and for irregularities as appropriate. Finally, essential cross-reference is made in the present list by means of the sign [→].

а	америка́нский
а́вгуст	англи́йский
авто́бус	англи́йский язы́к
автомоби́ль	англича́нин/-ча́нка
Аме́рика	А́нглия
америка́нец/-ка́нка	апре́ль

бабушка

бéгать, бежáть/по-

бéдный

без

бéлый

бéрег

библиотéка

билéт

благодарúть/по-

блúзко

блýзка

богáтый

бóлее

болéть

больнúца

больнóй

(бóльше → мнóго)

большóй

ботúнки

боя́ться

брат

брать/взять

бросáть/брóсить

брю́ки

бýдто

бýдущий

бумáга

буты́лка

бы

бывáть

бы́стро

быть, есть (нет)

в

вáжный

вáнна

ваш*

вверх

вдруг

ведь

вездé

(везтú → возúть)

век

велúкий

велосипéд

(вернýться → возвращáться)

вероя́тно

весёлый

веснá, веснóй

(вестú → водúть)

весь/вся/всё/все*

вéтер

вéчер, вéчером

вещь

(взять → брать)

вид

вúдеть(ся)/у-

вúлка

винó

виновáтый

висéть

включáть/-чúть

вкýсный

вмéсте

вниз, внизý

водá

водúть, вестú/по-

вóдка

возвращáться/-тúться,

   вернýться

вóздух

возúть, везтú/по-

во́зле
возмо́жно
война́
вокза́л
во́лосы
вообще́
вопро́с
восемна́дцать
во́семь
во́семьдесят
воскресе́нье
восьмо́й
вот
врач
вре́мя*
(всё, все → весь)
всегда́
всё-таки
встава́ть/встать
встреча́ть(ся)/встре́тить(ся)
всю́ду
вся́кий
вто́рник
второ́й
входи́ть/войти́
вчера́
вы
выключа́ть/вы́ключить
высо́кий
выходи́ть/вы́йти

газе́та
где
гла́вный
глаз
глу́пый

гляде́ть/по-
говори́ть/по-, сказа́ть
год
голова́
голубо́й
гора́
го́рло
го́род
горя́чий
гости́ница
гость
гото́вить/при-
гото́вый
грани́ца: за грани́цу/-цей
гро́мко
грузови́к
гря́зный
губа́
гуля́ть/по-

да
дава́ть/дать
давно́
да́же
далеко́, да́льше
два
двадца́тый
два́дцать
двена́дцать
дверь
двор
де́вочка
де́вушка
девяно́сто
девятна́дцать
девя́тый

де́вять
девятьсо́т
де́д(ушка)
дека́брь
де́лать/с-
де́ло
день, днём
день рожде́ния
де́ньги
дере́вня
де́рево
держа́ть
деся́тый
де́сять
(де́ти → ребёнок)
дива́н
дире́ктор
дли́нный
для
(днём → день)
до
до́брый
дово́льно
дождь
до́ктор
до́лго
до́лжен
дом
до́ма, домо́й
доро́га
дорого́й
доска́
дочь*
друг
друг дру́га
друго́й

ду́мать/по-
душ
дя́дя

его́
едва́
её
е́здить, е́хать/по-
е́сли
есть (+ → быть)
(е́хать → е́здить)
ещё

жаке́т
жа́лко, жаль
жа́рко
жда́ть/подо-
же
жела́ть/по-
желе́зная доро́га
жёлтый
жена́
же́нщина
живо́тное
жить
журна́л

за
забыва́ть/забы́ть
заво́д
за́втра
за́втракать/по-
закрыва́ть/закры́ть
закры́тый
замеча́ть/заме́тить
занима́ться
за́пах

затем
заходи́ть/зайти́
заче́м
звать/по-, как зову́т
звезда́
звони́ть/по-
звук
здесь
здоро́вый
здра́вствуй(те)
зелёный
земля́
зе́ркало
зима́, зимо́й
знако́мый
знать
зна́чить
зо́нтик
зуб

и
игра́ть
иде́я
(идти́ → ходи́ть)
из
изве́стный
извиня́ть/-ни́ть
из-за
изуча́ть/-чи́ть
и́ли
име́ть
и́мя*
ина́че
иногда́
иностра́нный
интере́сный

интересова́ть(ся)/за-
иска́ть
их
ию́ль
ию́нь

к
ка́ждый
каза́ться/по-, ка́жется
как
како́й
ка́мень
кани́кулы
каранда́ш
карма́н
ка́рта
карти́н(к)а
карто́фель, карто́шка
ка́сса
кассе́та
кварти́ра
кило́
киломе́тр
кино́
класс
класть/положи́ть
ключ
кни́га
когда́
колхо́з
кома́нда
коне́ц
коне́чно
конто́ра
конце́рт
конча́ть(ся)/ко́нчить(ся)

копе́йка
коро́ва
коро́ткий
корреспонде́нт/-ка
кото́рый
ко́фе
ко́фточка
ко́шка
краси́вый
кра́сный
кре́сло
крича́ть/за-, кри́кнуть
кро́ме
круго́м
кто
куда́
купа́ться
(купи́ть → покупа́ть)
кури́ть/по-, за-
курс
ку́ртка
кусо́к
ку́хня

ла́мпа
ле́вый
лёгкий, легко́
лёд
лежа́ть
лека́рство
ле́кция
лени́вый
лес
ле́стница
лета́ть, лете́ть/по-
ле́то, ле́том

(лечь → ложи́ться)
ли
лист
лифт
лицо́
лови́ть/пойма́ть
ло́дка
ложи́ться/лечь
ло́жка
лома́ть(ся)/с-
ло́шадь
луна́
(лу́чше, лу́чший → хоро́ший)
люби́мый
люби́ть/по-
(лю́ди → челове́к)

магази́н
май
ма́ленький
ма́ло, ме́ньше
ма́льчик
ма́рка
март
ма́сло
матема́тика
мать*
маши́на
ме́дленно
ме́жду
ме́нее
(ме́ньше → ма́ло)
ме́сто
ме́сяц
метро́
милиционе́р

90

милиция
милый
мимо
минута
мир
много, больше
может быть
можно
мой*
молодой
молоко
молчать
море
мороз
Москва
мост
мотоцикл
мочь/с-
муж
мужчина
музей
музыка
мы
мыть(ся)/вы-
мясо

на
наверх, наверху
над
надевать/надеть
надеяться
надо, нужно
назад: тому назад
называться
наконец
налево

направо
например
народ
настоящий
наука
находить(ся)/найти
начало
начинать(ся)/начать(ся)
наш*
не
небо
небольшой
недавно
недалеко
неделя
некоторый
нельзя
немного
несколько
(нести → носить)
нет (+ → быть)
ни … ни …
нигде
никакой
никогда
никто
никуда
ничто, ничего
но
новости
новый
нога
нож
ноль, нуль
номер
нос

носи́ть, нести́/по-
ночь, но́чью
ноя́брь
нра́виться/по-
ну
(ну́жно → на́до)
ну́жный
(нуль → ноль)

о
о́ба
обе́д, по́сле обе́да
обе́дать/по-
обеща́ть
о́блако
о́браз
объясня́ть/-ни́ть
обыкнове́нно, обы́чно
обяза́тельно
о́вощи
овца́
ого́нь
огро́мный
одева́ться/оде́ться
оди́н*
оди́ннадцать
одна́жды
одна́ко
о́зеро
окно́
о́коло
октя́брь
он/она́/оно́/они́*
опя́ть
о́сень, о́сенью
осо́бенно

остава́ться/оста́ться
остана́вливаться/
  останови́ться
остано́вка
осторо́жно
о́стров
от
отве́т
отвеча́ть/отве́тить
оте́ц
открыва́ть/откры́ть
откры́тый
отку́да
о́тпуск
о́тчество
о́чень
очки́
ошиба́ться/-би́ться
оши́бка

па́дать/упа́сть
паке́т
па́лец
пальто́
папиро́са
парк
парохо́д
па́рта
пе́рвый
переводи́ть/-вести́
пе́ред
перестава́ть/-ста́ть
переходи́ть/перейти́
перча́тка
пе́сня
петь/с-, за-

печка, печь
пиани́но
пи́во
пиджа́к
пионе́р/-ка
писа́ть/на-
письмо́
пить/вы́-
пла́вать, плыть
пла́кать/за-
пласти́нка
плати́ть/за-
пла́тье
плохо́й, пло́хо, ху́же
(плыть → пла́вать)
по
по-англи́йски/-ру́сски
повторя́ть/-ри́ть
пого́да
под
поднима́ть(ся)/подня́ть(ся)
подру́га
подходи́ть/подойти́
по́езд
пое́здка
пожа́луйста
пожива́ть
по́здно
(пойма́ть → лови́ть)
пока́
пока́зывать/показа́ть
покупа́ть/купи́ть
пол
по́лдень
по́ле
по́лночь

по́лный
полови́на
(положи́ть → класть)
получа́ть/-чи́ть
полчаса́
по́мнить/вс-
помога́ть/помо́чь
понеде́льник
понима́ть/поня́ть
пора́
по́сле
после́дний
посте́ль
посыла́ть/посла́ть
пото́м
потому́ что
похо́ж
почему́
по́чта
почти́
поэ́тому
пра́вда
пра́вый
пра́здник
предме́т
пре́жде
прекра́сный
при
приезжа́ть/-е́хать
принима́ть/-ня́ть
приноси́ть/-нести́
приходи́ть(ся)/прийти́(сь)
прия́тный
про
про́бовать/по-
проводи́ть/-вести́

продава́ть/-да́ть
проси́ть/по-
(прости́ть → проща́ть)
про́сто
про́тив
про́шлый
проща́ть/прости́ть
пря́мо
пти́ца
пуло́вер
пусто́й
пусть
путь
пятна́дцать
пя́тница
пя́тый
пять
пятьдеся́т

рабо́та
рабо́тать
рабо́чий
ра́вный: всё равно́
рад
ра́дио
раз
разбива́ть(ся)/-би́ть(ся)
ра́зве
раздева́ться/-де́ться
ра́зный
ра́но, ра́ньше
расска́зывать/-сказа́ть
ребёнок, де́ти
револю́ция
ре́зать/по-, от-
река́

рестора́н
реша́ть/реши́ть
род
роди́тели
роди́ться
Росси́я
рост
рот
руба́шка
рубль
рука́
ру́сский, ру́сская
ру́сский язы́к
ру́чка
ры́ба
ры́нок
ря́дом

с
сад
сади́ться/сесть
сам*
самолёт
са́мый
са́хар
све́жий
свет
свети́ть
свида́ние, до свида́ния
свобо́дный
свой*
себя́
сего́дня
седьмо́й
сейча́с
село́

семна́дцать
семь
се́мьдесят
семья́
сентя́брь
серди́ться/рас-
середи́на
се́рый
сестра́
(сесть → сади́ться)
сиде́ть
си́льный
си́ний
(сказа́ть → говори́ть)
ско́лько
ско́ро
ску́чный
сла́бый
сле́дующий
сли́шком
слова́рь
сло́во
слу́чай
случа́ться/-чи́ться
слу́шать/по-
слы́шать/у-
смешно́й
смея́ться/за-, рас-
смотре́ть/по-
снача́ла
снег
снима́ть/снять
сно́ва
соба́ка
сове́тский
Сове́тский Сою́з

совсе́м
согла́сен
со́лнце
соль
сон
со́рок
сосе́д/-ка
СССР
спа́льня
спаси́бо
спать
спина́
споко́йный
спорт
спра́шивать/спроси́ть
спуска́ться/спусти́ться
спустя́
сра́зу
среда́
среди́
ста́вить/по-
стака́н
станови́ться/стать
ста́нция
стара́ться/по-
ста́рый, ста́рший
(стать → станови́ться)
стена́
сто
сто́ить
стол
столо́вая
сторона́
стоя́ть
страна́
страни́ца

стра́нный
стра́шный
студе́нт/-ка
стул
суббо́та
су́мка
суп
сходи́ть/сойти́
счастли́вый
сын
сыр
сюда́

так
та́кже
тако́й
такси́
там
танцева́ть
таре́лка
та́ять/рас-
твой*
теа́тр
телеви́зор
телефо́н
те́ло
тёмный, темно́
тепе́рь
тёплый, тепло́
теря́ть/по-
тетра́дь
тётя
ти́хий
-то/-нибудь: како́й-, кто-,
    что-
това́рищ

тогда́
то́ есть
то́же
то́лстый
то́лько
то́нкий
тот/та/то/те*
трава́
тра́ктор
трамва́й
тре́тий*
три
три́дцать
трина́дцать
тролле́йбус
тру́дный, тру́дно
туда́
тума́н
тут
ту́фли
ты
ты́сяча
тяжёлый

у
у́гол
удава́ться/уда́ться
уже́
у́жинать/по-
узнава́ть/узна́ть
у́лица
улыба́ться/улыбну́ться
уме́ть/с-
умира́ть/умере́ть
у́мный
университе́т

(упа́сть → па́дать)
уро́к
успе́х
устава́ть/уста́ть
у́тро, у́тром
у́хо
уходи́ть/уйти́
уче́бник
учени́к/-и́ца
учёный
учи́тель/-ница
учи́ть(ся)/на-

фами́лия
февра́ль
фе́рма
фильм
фотоаппара́т
фотогра́фия
фру́кты

хвата́ть/хвати́ть
хлеб
ходи́ть, идти́/пойти́
холо́дный, хо́лодно
хоро́ший, хорошо́, лу́чше/-
    ший
хоте́ть(ся)/за-
хотя́
(ху́же → плохо́й)

цвет
цвето́к
це́лый
центр
це́рковь

чай
час
ча́сто
часть
часы́
ча́шка
чей*
челове́к, лю́ди
чем
чемода́н
че́рез
чёрный
четве́рг
четвёртый
че́тверть
четы́ре
четы́рнадцать
число́
чи́стый
чита́ть/про-
что
что́бы
чу́вствовать (себя́)
чуть

ша́пка
шестна́дцать
шесто́й
шесть
шестьдеся́т
ше́я
широ́кий
шко́ла
шу́ба
шум

97

щека́

экза́мен
эта́ж
э́тот/э́та/э́то/э́ти*

ю́бка

я
язы́к
яйцо́
янва́рь
я́ркий
я́сный